Something for
the Weekend

Something for the Weekend

The Collected Columns of Sir Terry Wogan

TERRY WOGAN

An Orion paperback

First published in Great Britain in 2013
by Orion
This paperback edition published in 2015
by Orion Books Ltd,
Carmelite House, 50 Victoria
Embankment, London EC4Y 0DZ
An Hachette UK company

7 9 10 8 6

A CIP catalogue record for this book is available
from the British Library.

ISBN 978-1-4091-4880-7

Typeset at The Spartan Press Ltd,
Lymington, Hants

Printed and bound by CPI Group (UK) Ltd,
Croydon, CR0 4YY

The Orion Publishing Group's policy is to use papers that
are natural, renewable and recyclable products and made
from wood grown in sustainable forests. The logging and
manufacturing processes are expected to conform to the
environmental regulations of the country of origin.

www.orionbooks.co.uk

For Helen. Always.

ACKNOWLEDGEMENTS

I suppose you think it's easy pounding out this stuff, week in, week out? You're right. Particularly because of the enthusiastic encouragement I've had from indulgent editors and the gentle guidance of kindly journalists who've never once taken the scissors to my efforts. It's been a pleasure and a privilege to work with them – for a great newspaper. And to have it all enhanced by the *Telegraph*'s greatest of all cartoonists: Matt . . .

CONTENTS

WELCOME! . . .

This fragrant nosegay of pithy pars has been lightly culled from a weekly column on the back page of the Sunday Telegraph, *shrewdly titled 'Wogan's World'. There are a couple of longer pieces that may test your patience, but most are mercifully short, pursuing the old adage of brevity being the soul of wit, that also panders to my own brief attention span. It's my feeling that whatever's bothering you, you ought to be able to say it in less than 500 words. The rest is window-dressing . . . Probably explains why I didn't write* War and Peace . . .

THE GHOSTS OF CHRISTMAS

It is a truth universally acknowledged that in some dusty corner of every home there stands an unused exercise bicycle with five miles on the clock. In every larder you will find a boxed, unopened panettone cake, pressed into your hands by the proprietor of an Italian restaurant three Christmases ago. Over there a SodaStream fizzy drinks maker from the 1970s takes up space with a tin of Golden Syrup four years past its sell-by date.

New arrivals over the last couple of years are the bread and ice cream-makers, patiently awaiting their second use. And look! Gathering its first cobweb, the juicer. With what pride we took it home, eager for the health-giving goodness it would bring to our tired bodies. It took eight oranges to make a half glass. Over the top, even for the most health-conscious. But that wasn't what spelt the juicer's death. It was the washing-up. It takes 10 minutes of hard graft to clear the gunk out of a juicer. And life's too short to stuff a mushroom . . .

One of my listeners claims to have invented a device called 'The Smugometer', which will give an early warning of Christmas cards containing 'family newsletters'. The present Mrs Wogan and I are proud of our children, but always feel inadequate when reading of the phenomenal achievements of other families. Faultless and brilliant, they stride through life without a hiccup. Couldn't we declare a moratorium on these things? Or send newsletters of our own, along the lines of: 'Young Timmy has finished his second stretch on the Moor; little Nancy is off the meths for the present and dear Kylie is doing community service for stabbing her teacher. There go our hopes of Oxbridge.'

19 December 2004

WAVE OF DESTRUCTION

Pestilence, plague, disaster, disease: not so long ago all God's doing. Now, everything bad that happens is Man's fault. Isn't it time we laid the blame squarely where it belongs, at the feet of Mother Nature, who's been single-mindedly trying to knock us off ever since we got here?

The shock of the southern Asian tsunami and its seemingly endless horror took the world by surprise. Its enormity seemed to take an age to sink in . . . and just as we were enjoying our yearly Season of Over-Indulgence. In 2004, we spent about £270 billion in cash and roughly the same amount on credit cards. The Government has pledged £50 million to help the victims. How much is enough? As ever the British public has responded magnificently to the appeal for help, and their contributions will match – if not better – the Government's. As I know from 25 years of Children in Need, with the British public, you only have to ask.

It's not easy being Charlie Chuckles when disaster strikes, which is why, in a cowardly way, I've been grateful to be away from the microphone this week. Light-hearted banter is difficult in the face of dreadful news, particularly as it grows worse and worse with each passing day. Of course, it's necessary to keep the best side out; remaining cheerful in the face of adversity: keeping a sense of humour in terrible circumstances is one of this nation's shining attributes. Another is its extraordinary tolerance. When the terrible news of the Birmingham pub bombings was broadcast, I had to follow it with a cheerful Irish voice. Now, it wasn't my fault, nor that of any decent Irish person, but still . . . not one letter of hate did I receive, not even a complaint.

Years later, somebody did send a bomb to the BBC with my name on it. The police stopped the traffic from Portland Place to

4

Oxford Circus. Luckily, the thing was pretty harmless and swiftly disarmed. The parcel bomber could scarcely have been called a loyal listener, though. I was on holiday when he tried to blow me up. I didn't know whether to be relieved or piqued . . .

2 January 2005

AUNTIE

Late last year I was privileged to present awards to the BBC's unsung heroes: the engineers, the sound men, the cameramen, the technicians – the real BBC. Each winner received as their prize a slate from the Broadcasting House roof, now no longer with us.

'A slate!' you sneer, 'I've heard that Auntie was tightening her stays, but this smacks of cheese-paring.' There is much in what you say, and good husbandry is the watchword of the Corporation these days. Still, those slates, those slivers of broadcasting history, reminded me of my early days as a boy broadcaster, when from the window of my dingy little studio I could observe the morning doings on the BBC roof. There, the very parapet from which middle management hurled old Nolan Sisters records to repel disgruntled listeners. Across the shining slates, the gaily striped canopies of Birt's Bistro were alive with the merry pop of the champagne cork. And on every second Thursday, the Dance of the BBC Virgins . . .

This was a ritual whose origins are lost in the mists of time, although it was said that the great Reith himself had officiated as High Priest on more than one occasion, dressed in a toga, his noble brow wreathed in marjoram and thyme. Supplications were offered to Auriel, the Ear in the Sky, and the dancing bordered on the tempestuous, according to the recently discovered diaries of Alvar Lidell. The trouble was that by the time my innocent eyes got to take a peek, the Dance of the BBC Virgins was a sad relic of a once-great past. As I was duty-bound to point out to my listeners, no one ever turned up.

I might have forgotten all about it if I hadn't been accosted in a blood-boltered corridor of Broadcasting House by one of those formidable BBC Ladies whose job was to strike terror into all who crossed the threshold of the old Temple to the Arts.

'You,' she thundered, 'imply that there are no virgins in the BBC. Well, there are. And I am one!' Turning heavily on a blue-stockinged heel, she strode off. I felt like a Viking who had been burnt before he'd pillaged.

9 January 2005

THE GREAT AND THE GOOD

To the Palace then, and a grand levee to honour the great and the good, and many a reformed reprobate, of the British music industry, which has brought much glory to Britain and, more importantly, much gold to her coffers. Everywhere you look in the gilded halls, a famous face, with voice to match. We line up to meet Her Majesty and Prince Philip, and I observe the 'Royal Effect': otherwise confident, successful people begin to behave in a highly strung, nervous manner. The only one unaffected is Dame Vera Lynn, but then she's been an unofficial royal since the last Unpleasantness. The Queen and the Prince enter, attempting to put even the most fretful at ease.

As Her Majesty leaves, Phil Collins whistles the five notes from *Close Encounters of the Third Kind*. The Queen turns, smiling. 'That was nice,' she says, 'What was it?' Collins is speechless. 'He was trying to get in touch with ET, Ma'am,' I gabble. The Queen smiles in a kindly way, and moves on. Phil Collins, distraught, turns to me. 'Why did I do that? What came over me?' I shudder. The Royal Effect has struck again.

The 'Delia Effect' is something else, and hitherto has manifested itself in enormous upsurges in the sales of cranberries and sea salt. However, the good Delia's bravura performance at Norwich City FC last week gave a whole new meaning to the phenomenon. It now seems closely to resemble the Royal Effect, inducing as it does irrational behaviour in otherwise sensible people, and a stunned silence from the onlookers.

On related matters, an observant listener has spotted the current vogue for seeing likenesses of the famous in food. Mother Teresa has been seen in a biscuit, and various icons have turned up in everything from rice puddings to a bar of soap. Only last week, someone saw the image of their dead dog in a loaf of bread.

As my listener dished up the Sunday roast a week ago, she was astonished to see an uncanny resemblance to myself in a Yorkshire pudding. I've got first refusal, otherwise it goes on eBay.

6 March 2005

EUROVISION

And so to Kyiv (only the chicken is Kiev), capital of the Ukraine, the old Soviet bread basket; say what you like, I've got to see the world with the Eurovision Song Contest . . . well, of late, that part of the world that used to be part of the old Soviet bloc. Ever since the Balkan and Baltic states were allowed to enter, it has become less of a song contest and more of an old pals act. The West won the Cold War but lost the Eurovision.

What could the discerning Western music lover have made of Ukraine's own entry by Greenjolly, *Razom Nas Bahato (Together We're Many)*? It was the anthem of the Orange Revolution that swept Viktor Yushchenko to power late last year. Maybe Britain should try entering *Jerusalem* next year.

It is not the first political statement made at the Eurosong. Years ago in Stockholm, when the Portuguese made their entry on stage with a carnation sticking from the barrel of a gun, it was a signal to those at home to start the revolution that overthrew the dictator Antonio Salazar. Then there was Luxembourg, after the Munich Olympics massacre, when the audience were warned not to stand up to applaud lest they be shot by security guards. There wasn't much of an atmosphere that year, as I recall . . .

By the time you read this, the Ukraine will be slowly returning to sanity. From the Black Sea coast to the Russian border, they descended in their thousands on their capital city, as if in a great pilgrimage. Those unlucky enough not to have a tent slept in the parks, in alleyways and doorways. For all of the Ukraine has lived for last night, ever since that sturdy girl in the leather skirt with the whip won Eurovision for them last year.

Just as the winners of the two previous years, Estonia and Latvia, Ukraine saw Eurovision as its chance to show the world that it was free at last from oppression and totalitarianism. For those of us for whom democracy is taken for granted, the Eurovision Song Contest may seem like a grandiose musical mediocrity. To the people of the Ukraine, it was a hymn to freedom.

22 May 2005

DIGGING AROUND

It seems that each week brings exciting news of ground-breaking discoveries from the prehistoric past: for instance, an ancestor who was strolling around millions of years earlier than previously thought. This on the basis of a shard of skull with a hole at the back at an angle the researchers think indicates that the fellow was walking about on his own two feet. Then there are the bones found on a remote Indonesian island that provide incontrovertible evidence to researchers of a furry little manikin, not unlike a Hobbit. Who can forget that television series on dinosaurs, with the giant flightless parrot with feathers and a blue beak that terrorised all about it? A leather sandal, dating back to the Iron Age, has just been found, possibly indicating that in those far-off days man had only one leg . . . now we hear of a dinosaur that looked like Edward Scissorhands. A friend has rearranged the bones left over from his dinner, added a black beret, and claims to have discovered a creature that looks like Frank Spencer. He's calling it a 'Doyouthinktheyllfundus' . . .

To cap a week bursting with palaeontological good things, Sir David Attenborough rejoiced in a pine tree from the Jurassic period with, we are told, a 'bubbly chocolate bark'. Much further along the path of Time's winged chariot, they still don't know who or what killed young King Tut, but research may show that it was murder. Or a broken leg. Or something. At least we now know what the little chap looked like. Thank heaven, I was sick with worry.

A correspondent takes exception to the casual bandying about by politicians of the word 'billion'. He's worked out a few 'billion' facts: a billion seconds ago, it was 1959. A billion minutes ago, Jesus was still alive. A billion hours ago, our ancestors were struggling with the Iron Age, probably on one leg. A billion days ago, they still hadn't got to their feet. And a billion pounds ago, was eight hours 20 minutes . . . at the rate the Government spends.

15 May 2005

JETSET

As far as airlines are concerned, less is more: the less you pay, the more the delay, discomfort, congestion and lack of service. But it's not just the cheapo carriers; I've travelled on two national airlines recently for exorbitant fares and on both there were delays, overcrowding and non-existent service. The slowest cabin crew in the history of flight took me to Vienna, and it was an hour and a quarter before they served anybody anything. Following an announcement extolling the virtues of their distinguished chef, who had prepared for us a delicious 'balanced' meal, we were finally dished up two meatballs and mash.

I travelled back from Shannon on another national carrier that now serves you nothing, cleverly avoiding the need for 'balance'. Apart from trundling a trolley of sandwiches and drinks that nobody wanted to pay for, the cabin crew had nothing to do, passing their time chattering loudly. As soon as the plane landed, half of them were off before the passengers were out of their seats.

Still on the subject of travel, rarely has any topic provoked such a reaction from my listeners as the news that rail fares are to rise steeply because people are using the trains too much. This on top of the congestion charges, planned road tolls and fuel price increases because we're using the roads too much. Now the Government wants more land to build more homes so more people will use the roads and the trains. I think I'll get my coat . . .

Would that there were some other way to go places. 'What about the balloon?' I hear you cry, and you're leaning against an open door with me there. Nobody has explained satisfactorily to me why, if you want to see the world, you can't go straight up in a balloon and hover until your chosen destination arrives beneath you. If the earth is truly spinning on its axis, surely it would be simplicity itself to park your balloon on the correct latitude and wait for, say, Bermuda, to make its way around to you. Then, a graceful descent to a pink, sandy beach. Holiday over, up we go again and in a matter of hours there's dear old Blighty awaiting our return. I'm amazed Branson hasn't thought of it.

26 June 2005

DOUBLE DUTCH

A listener off to Syria phoned the Post Office currency service. Big mistake. 'Which currency do you require?'

'I don't know what it is called, but I'm looking for the currency for Syria.'

'Where, madam?'

'Syria.'

'Is that the name of the currency?'

'No, the country.'

'Are you sure, madam?'

'Yes. The country is called Syria.'

'And where is this, er, Syria?'

'The Middle East.'

'Where, madam?'

'The Middle East. Not too far from Iraq, the one we invaded with the Americans. Can you help me or not?'

'So you want to buy a currency called Syria for a country called the Middle East. Let me speak to my line manager.' Long pause. 'Madam, we have checked our lists and there is no such country as Syria. I suggest you contact your travel agent to find out where you are really going.' End of call.

Another listener, on hearing this, excused the Post Office because they are somewhat behind the times and probably only know Syria by its former name, Assyria. To get there, you head across the Roman empire to Constantinople, there to board a trireme to cross to the empire of the Hittites. Then, south-west towards Babylon, hanging a left for Assyria. When you see a bloke with a square beard, you're there . . .

'Have you got these in a bigger size?' A question put recently by a customer in a shoe shop. The assistant looked doubtful. 'What, both of them?' A friend, buying a tablecloth, asked if it was reversible. 'No, but you can use both sides.' 'These can be used three months from today,' said the assistant with the voucher book. Pause. 'That will be, er . . .' – 'November,' my correspondent helpfully said. Another pause. The girl turned to her colleague: 'How do you spell November?' There were three vouchers, the operation took some time. Good job it wasn't February.

I offer these examples, of which I have enough to girdle the planet, in a month in which the best exam results ever have been recorded.

28 August 2005

PIDGIN ENGLISH

News that they are going to re-route pigeon races in Ireland to avoid airports raises the question: who's going to tell the pigeons? Are they planning to attach little signposts to balloons and float them up in the vicinity of airports with 'No Entry' in pidgin English?

In these politically correct times, the euphemism has come into its own: the elderly are now 'senior citizens', their forgetfulness a 'senior moment'. A friend, hurrying around a store frantic to just buy and get out in the traditional male manner, noticed a new type of trouser billed as having an 'active waistband'. Infinitely preferable, of course, to saying that they are designed for the 'fuller figure', and definitely better than saying 'fat boys' kecks'. People who buy 'active waistband' slacks haven't got a waist to begin with, and to describe them as 'active' leans towards hyperbole.

Everyone has a tale to tell of the apparent inability to spell of large sections of the community. Only this week I heard of a recent 'gail' warning flashed on Scottish television screens, and from an officer in Guildford police station of a young miscreant protesting at the custody desk: 'You're fick, all ov you. FICK!' To emphasise the point, the lad spelt it out. 'You're stupid. S.T.O.O.P.I.D. all ov you.'

A silent prayer for the woman in a supermarket in Inverness who asked for the 100 bonus reward points offered for any purchase of organic meat. The young lady assistant flatly refused to oblige. She was adamant:

'Bonus points only for organic lamb, beef or pork, madam. Sorry.'

'But this is organic bacon,' protested the customer.

'Sorry, madam, it must be lamb, beef, or pork . . .'

4 September 2005

THE GOOD LIFE

Many years ago, we took a family holiday on Hydra in the Greek Islands and a hydrofoil took us there from the port of Athens. A calm journey over the wine-dark sea, and then, our luggage loaded on a couple of donkeys, we made our climb up the appropriately named 'Donkey-shit Lane' to our rented villa, where the terrace provided a beautiful view of Hydra's harbour. It was an idyllic setting, marred only by the attitude of the woman the owners had left in charge, who guarded every pot, plant and piece of furniture like a Doberman. Still, she was a decent enough cook, and had a winning way with a meatball, so our little group was well content.

Every day, my then small children and I would watch the little boats come and go beneath us, and then, one day, came a private yacht so big that it was unable to enter the narrow harbour and it moored outside. It was a magnificent vessel. I took my children down to see it, to admire more closely the fruits of wealth, to catch a glimpse of how the other half lived. It was pristine white, about 100-feet long, and had two decks and a luxurious sitting area on the stern, where the proud owners sipped the regulatory cocktails seemingly oblivious to an admiring throng. All was glass and brass, and it bristled with state-of-the-art sonar and radar.

There were even two speedboats attached to the sides, and a deck from which these lotus eaters could swim, if they ever tore themselves away from the foie gras and pink champagne. On all sides, brisk young men in crisp white uniforms rushed to the passengers' bidding, and I reflected, as I made my weary way back up the 300 steps of Donkey-shit Lane, that if ever there was a shrieking example of 'the good life', those lucky people on that shiny big boat were living it.

The children were all excitement as they described this

19

magnificent palace-on-the-sea to their mother, and naturally the following morning they were up early onto the terrace to see if it was still there. It was; but there was something even more exciting, which they dragged me out of bed to see. It was another ship, moored beside the marvellous yacht. Only this one was 2000-feet long.

We rushed down the lane and onto the harbour wall. This was also a yacht, three times bigger and better in every way than the one it was dwarfing, the one we'd admired so much. This enormous gin palace had three decks, four launches, a swimming pool, several decks for lounging, innumerable electronic gizmos and a helicopter-landing pad, with helicopter. There were languid people on every deck, lounging, sipping, nibbling, laughing – and why wouldn't they be? No sign of life at all on what we now called the Little Boat, and my heart went out to its owner.

Just think of it: you make a ton of money, you're the talk of the town, the toast of your friends and family. From here on in it's first-class all the way, the best hotels, the best tables, the bowing and scraping of maître d's, the Bentley Continental, the house in the Boltons and the yacht. Ah, the yacht. Several million pounds'-worth, a fortune to run, but worth it, dammit, to sail yourself and your friends around the Med, to moor by the millionaires' watering hole and sip champagne while pretending not to notice the envious, admiring glances of less fortunate passers-by.

And then, one terrible evening as you contentedly lay by a little island, just off the Grecian mainland, something far bigger and better and more expensive than you know you will ever afford plonks itself right down beside you. Of all the harbours, watering holes and islands in the world, this huge thing has to pick yours . . .

The little yacht was gone the following morning, to no one's surprise. I hope it found another place where the ships were smaller, where people would still pass it by in open-mouthed admiration, but I knew things would never be the same for its owner. The magic was gone, the champagne soured, pride irredeemably deflated. He'd learnt the hard way the lesson that only a fool ignores. Just when you think you've achieved the good life, up comes somebody else with a better one.

Meanwhile, that man with the big yacht outside Hydra harbour is bound to meet his nemesis, as he bestrides the Med like a colossus. Chelsea's owner, Roman Abramovich, for example, can boast three ships bigger than his, and then there are the Saudi princes . . .

I'll bet George Clooney was congratulating himself that it 'doesn't get any better than this' when I watched him disport himself around the pool at the Grand Hotel du Cap in Antibes a couple of summers ago. What he didn't know was that it does, and I was getting it. I'd sailed up to the hotel in a tender from one of the loveliest yachts in the world, Sir Don Gosling's *Leander*, and as I sipped a cocktail in the bar, and looked down on George, a hint of a superior smile may have played, just for a moment, on my lips.

What's so hot about 'the good life' anyway? Good is just OK, average, could do better. Why aspire to something that's only one step up from mediocre? Why not 'the best life'? We've lost the meaning of the word 'good'. To be 'good' used to mean to be well behaved, decent, virtuous, God-fearing. 'Be a good boy now' in my youth meant not running around like a mad thing getting dirt all over your clothes; it meant sitting up straight and eating your vegetables. The message from Church, teachers and parents alike was that you were meant to strive to be good in all aspects of your life, to please God and be a credit to your parents.

Now it's: 'Be good to yourself – because you're worth it.' Meaning, love yourself, pamper yourself – the watchword of the 'Me, Me, Me' generation. The very antithesis of what I was brought up to believe: self-praise is no praise, vanity is a sin, and you're not worth tuppence until you've done something worthwhile. Nobody aspires to goodness in that sense any more, it seems. If you want to live 'the good life' you've got to be famous or rich. It's what the word 'wannabe' was invented for, it's why people are lining up to be degraded in front of millions on reality TV shows. They don't know that fame doesn't bring happiness, that in these days of obsessive media interest, fame works in inverse proportion to happiness: the more famous you are, the less your chances of contentment and peace.

Contentment and peace would be my definition of the 'good life'; together with joy, of course. The joy of having your family around you, the indescribable joy of a first grandchild, the satisfaction of knowing that your children are so close to each other, the warmth and love of the woman who has been by your side for more than 40 years. Even then these joys are fleeting, just as that ephemeral 'good life' is. You can't spend all your life sipping champagne on a yacht, while lesser mortals gaze in envy. Abramovich had to work hard, in the most inhospitable region of Siberia, to make his money. George Clooney and other big-name actors have to get out there, and act; and their reputation and fame are as fleeting as their last movie. They've got plenty of money, they could walk away from it all tomorrow and spend the rest of their days lotus-eating, living the life. You know that they won't. Like the rest of us, they'll enjoy a break, probably a great deal more luxurious than we can imagine, but being actors, after a couple of weeks, they'll begin to wonder why their agent hasn't called, even when they told him not to bother them. Another week and they'll be climbing the walls with insecurity – 'Get me off this boat, I want to work.'

I've never understood why talented people who have achieved recognition, fortune and 'the good life' want the world to know their name. They want their picture in the paper, they want to be able to ring up Gordon Ramsay whenever they want a table. The good life isn't good enough if nobody knows you're having it. I feel like shouting, 'For heaven's sake!', you've got it made, your dreams have come true, and nobody knows who you are, or what you look like. And all you really want is to have your photograph taken as you come out of the Ivy. There goes happiness, there goes peace, and you'll never know privacy again.

Fame and its trappings are what most would equate with the good life; for others it would be riches, but for many it would be power, the kind of influence that makes others pay attention, cater to your every whim, jump every time you snap your fingers. Television performers get treated like this: 'Is Terry OK? Are those flowers in his dressing room? Get him a cup of coffee, see if he wants anything . . .'

In the seventies, there was no need for soul-searching; the good life was crystal clear. It was Tom and Barbara Good – Richard Briers and Felicity Kendal – on the television. Self-sufficient, frugal, never knowing where the next penny was coming from, living on love. A wonderful example of middle-class thrift, and its admirable values. Yet, over the run of the series, it was the couple next door who won the hearts and minds of those who aspired to the good life. Margot and Jerry, he a businessman under the thumb of his bossy, pretentious wife who spent all her time at coffee mornings, ladies' lunches and the drama group, wasting all of Jerry's hard-earned on designer dresses and curtains. And the public loved her. That was 'the good life' they were after. It was ever thus and always will be; but it doesn't work in 'the real life'.

4 September 2005

THE NOB WITH THE GOB

The good news that Bob Geldof is to be given the freedom of the city of Dublin prompted me to speculate that it was only a matter of time before they raised a statue to himself. A risky move, given Dubliners' habit of nicknaming their public monuments. The one to Molly Malone ('Alive, Alive Oh') is popularly known as the 'Tart with the Cart'. Anna Livia, the Liffey goddess, is the 'Floozie in the Jacuzzi'. The tall, spike-like structure that replaced Nelson in O'Connell Street is the 'Stiletto in the Ghetto', and I'll not trouble you with what they call the statues of James Joyce and Oscar Wilde.

The suggestions for Bob were many and varied, but only one was suitable for family reading. He is depicted offering food to the needy so it will be dubbed 'The Oaf with the Loaf'. In my own case, it was thought that my recent elevation to the lower ranks of the nobility would inevitably result in my own likeness being jeered as 'The Nob with the Gob'.

Which reminds me, that's what television journalists call presenters: Gobs on Sticks. As a newsreader myself, in the quondam days of Irish television, I can only say that today's batch don't know they're born. It's all autocue nowadays, the news scrolling in the camera lens directly in the reader's eye-line. All that fiddling with bits of paper and a computer is window dressing.

In the bad old days, you fiddled nervously with the paper because the news was printed on it, and you read it with your head bobbing up and down like a nodding dog in a car's back window. Then the floor manager would hold up a sign: 'Drop next item. Go to Berlin.' You calmly ditched the next sheet and then, with increasing fear, searched for 'Berlin'. Not there. Go through the sheaves again. Look up, smile at the camera. It's not there. You're sweating now. Where is it? Smile. The floor manager's waving, now everyone's panicking. Maybe it's in the reject pile? Thank God, it's there. The floor manager holds up a new sign: 'Drop Berlin. Go to Jerusalem.'

And you wonder why people don't watch television so intently these days . . .

11 September 2005

ROWING INTO TROUBLE

On a recent visit to Aberdeen, I was plied with the local delicacy, the rowie. Exiled Aberdonians, I was assured, have it flown to them all over the world, such is their craving for the thing. And if you like a lump of salty lard, you should join their club. Effete southern softie that I am, I didn't, and said so over the radio. The backlash from Scottish newspapers was immediate and ferocious, the headlines loudly condemning my 'outburst'. It was as if I had cast doubt on every Aberdonian's manhood, and impugned the virtue of his woman into the bargain. For heaven's sake, even the petulant French wouldn't throw such a hissy fit if I condemned the croissant.

Talking of which, an inhabitant of Nairn, 90 miles to the north of the Granite City, claims they make the best rowies by taking away much of the salt and substituting sugar, creating a kind of croissant. In Inverness it's known as a 'crozonk'. So, there you have it: the rowie actually hails from France. Let's see what a stushie that causes.

It is truly said that a presenter cannot open his mouth on radio or television without somebody, somewhere taking offence. Indeed I suspect that there is a hard core of listeners and viewers who sit by their appliances just waiting to be offended. A cheery 'Good Morning' offered innocently will be answered by a snarling 'What's good about it?' From now on, I may only approach Aberdeen under cover of darkness, but it had better join the queue of places where I'm already a pariah: Denmark, for instance, where the entire nation took my passing ribaldry on their Eurovision coverage as a foul slur on all that's best in Danish life. I wouldn't mind if they were paying a licence fee.

Or Hungary, which has got itself into a right old state, claiming that I have insulted Hungarians everywhere by calling them 'gypsies'. All I said was that the Hungarian entry in this year's Eurovision had a 'gypsy flavour', evoking memories of camp fires and tempestuous lovelies with flashing teeth and golden earrings. And if they think that's insulting, wait till they hear my views on goulash.

16 October 2005

CREDIT WHERE IT'S DUE

Given that I broadcast daily on BBC Radio 2, aka the Coffin-Dodgers' Network, it's inevitable that the latest rumpus over pensions would engage the attention of my listeners. There was excitement when the Pensions Minister said that, following the latest report, the Government would be taking the document around the country, speaking to the ordinary working man and getting his views. My listeners can hardly wait, as they have read the results of countless surveys, but never once been asked anything by anyone with a clipboard. They're a little unsure how to respond to the Minister's inquiry. Do they tell him that they will be happy with the same terms as an MP or public-service employee, or should they hold out for free beer for all workers, with mixed bathing for the unemployed?

More confusion, schism and doubt over tax credits. To the Government's chagrin, people just aren't claiming them. 'God knows,' a correspondent cries, 'I've tried.' He made a claim and received a reply stating that he hadn't sent the information required (without any indication of what the information required was), therefore he would invoke a charge of £1,000, which he would have to pay unless he made immediate contact.

Luckily, a telephone number was provided. It had a pre-recorded message: 'Please try later.' So, how can he find out what information is required, if he can't get through? How does he pay, if he needs to? How does he avoid paying? Is there an ombudsman in the house?

4 December 2005

ARISE, SIR TERRY

The thing is, nobody really cares. All they want to know is: 'What did she say to you?' After a hundred such queries it's hard not to answer: 'Hello, mush, here's your gong. Now clear off – don't want to be late for lunch . . .'

My loyal listeners (and Her Majesty's loyal subjects) were all concerned for my well-being at the hands of the sword-wielding monarch. One offered to tape back my ears, lest the cold steel leave a lobe on the Palace carpet, while another suggested a small but serviceable device not unlike a stairlift that would help me off my knees.

After my dangerous moment with the blade was shown on television, a worried mother wanted to know how the Queen gets all that swordplay past Health and Safety, when it's too dangerous for her own children to play conkers? This perceptive viewer also noticed that Dr Brian May of Queen (the pop group – do keep up), who was receiving a CBE for playing his guitar on the roof of the Palace in the biting wind, had blagged a Busby as a souvenir and wanted to know if I'd managed to nick anything, such as a bottle of Blue Nun, or a couple of teaspoons.

First of all, that's Brian's hair, and second, there was no strong drink. There wasn't any tea, not to mind spoons . . . No time, you see. Three hundred spectators to be corralled into the Ballroom, and 110 nervous wrecks to be rehearsed in the protocol of investiture. You think you can just walk out there, exchange the airy banter with Herself, trouser the gong, and off to the bar? There's no such thing as a free lunch (although, having been up since all hours of the morning, I could have done with a sustaining sausage roll or two) and there are no free rides at the Palace.

All those Beefeaters with their halberds, Gurkhas, chamberlains, equerries, commanders and colonels, Hussars in highly polished boots, haven't gone to all this trouble for some hobble-dehoy to swan in and out as if he owned the place, even if he has got into a frock coat and a top hat. Then there's the Orchestra of the Welsh Guards, running the gamut from Sinatra to Bach, who haven't come all the way from the Valleys for their own amusement. Although the pianist did seem to have a mind of his own.

If you're used to draughty, empty rooms in North Acton, or some freezing church hall in Barnet, the rehearsal room at the Palace is a definite step-up in class. Huge, vaulted, hung with drapes and grand portraits, chandeliers, and a generous daubing of gold leaf, it is well calculated to reduce even the most confident and self-regarding of worthy recipients to apprehensive shivers. In case you've forgotten who you are, this will get you back on the straight and narrow. A charming military man, in blinding boots and spurs, about seven feet tall, takes us through the routine. Come to the entrance; wait. When the shaking figure in front of you moves on towards Her Majesty, step forward a few wobbly paces and stand by the equerry. Chap in front gets a gong, backs off, white with fright. The man calls out your name.

This is it, forward a couple of paces, then turn to face the Queen; bow the head, not the body, kneel on the cushion, head up. Down comes the sword. Up you get, while they hand Her Maj the doings on a cushion. She hands them over. You speak when you're spoken to – not before. She's 'Your Majesty' and then 'Ma'am', as in 'jam', not 'warm'. When she extends the royal hand, that's it. Back a couple of paces, bow the head, exit stage left, perspiring gently with no feeling below your knees.

All of this while the orchestra is tootling away to Purcell and Porter. And 300 pairs of spectators' eyes are trained on the back of your neck, wondering what you've ever done to deserve this.

They are very jolly when they rehearse you, and I'm sure that it's meant to relax you when they recall all the previous unfortunates who have curtseyed when they should have bowed, forgotten to address the Queen correctly, turned right instead of left, spoken before they were spoken to, and continued to babble on after they'd got the royal handshake.

All that does is make you even more sick with worry, but when the Big Moment comes, it's all over so quickly you wonder if it has really happened. The Queen has the lightest of touches with the blade on both shoulders, she deftly pins on the insignia of Knight Commander, and hangs the Order of Knighthood round my neck.

Then she tells me she listened to me on the radio that morning, and I ask if she heard me read out a listener's offer of a sausage roll and a glass of Pinot if she'd agree to turn on the Christmas lights at Great Yarmouth on her way to Sandringham. She smiles, extends the hand, and I know it is time to back off. Bow and make myself scarce.

They lead me to the back of the hall and I watch as each of the other 100-plus deserving people is received with the same gracious courtesy and warm smile as the Queen has extended to me.

In an hour, it's all over. Her Majesty leaves, followed by Gurkhas and Beefeaters, and then we're all out in the courtyard of the Palace with the photographers and the camera crews, everybody linked by the occasion, smiling, congratulating each other, not wanting the Great Day to end . . . ever.

My family and friends then gather in a humble hostelry, and we enjoy a celebratory lunch. My wife's hat is a triumph, three grown-ups who used to be my children say warm, wonderful words that bring tears to the eyes, and they present me with my very own sword, on which have been engraved their names, and the date that their father became a Knight Commander and a Knight of the British Empire, never to be forgotten.

Not that a single person in that room, full of friends and family, will ever call him 'Sir' . . .

11 December 2005

SAY CHEESE

Beset on all sides, as we are, by a world gone mad, you may not have noticed how bad-tempered women are looking these days. Not all women, of course. Cherie Blair, for one, seems ever to be bursting into raucous laughter, but have you ever seen a super-model smile? They sway down the ramps of Paris, London, Milan and New York with legs looking like they'd be better off in a nest, and faces like thunder. Their scornful looks and aloof demeanour make it all too clear what they think of the paying customers – which doesn't seem to make a lot of commercial sense. Didn't some wise American philosopher, Colonel Sanders perhaps, or Ronald McDonald, say: 'Sell the sizzle not the steak'?

As for the shrews on the perfume ads, they look as if they'd claw your eyes out. They actually snarl, like felines with indigestion. Who wants to buy a scent that turns your beloved into the she-devil from hell?

Smiling's out, obviously, if you're selling a smell, but sucking up has never been out of fashion in ladies' lingerie. In an attempt to lure self-conscious men into ladies' underwear, a caring department store has appointed chaps to help other chaps overcome their natural reluctance to discuss the finer points of the kite gusset and whalebone corsets.

A friend braved the sneers of his peers and entered the store in a hangdog manner to liaise freely with a 'stocking feller'. (I know: probably another inspirational touch from the same ad agency that does perfume for Tasmanian she-devils.) The 'feller' handed my friend a list with questions: how would he describe the lady? A: Glamorous; B: Feminine; C: Flirty; D: Sassy? He chose 'Sassy'. From the second list he picked 'Party Girl', and from the third 'Catherine Zeta-Jones'.

After a moment's perusal, the 'stocking feller' looked at my friend in a knowing manner and said: 'These aren't for your wife . . . are they, sir?'

18 December 2005

SCENT OF A WOMAN

Returning from a bracing week in the shadow of the Pyrenees, the first British newspaper I pick up boasts the headline: 'Why does my sweat smell of urine?' Then, on another page, a photo of Sarah Miles, the actress whose name is never mentioned without the obligatory reference to her habit of downing two pints of her own urine every day. Now, I have been accused of taking the aforementioned bodily by-product from time to time, but, refreshed and revived by my holiday, this kind of rough talk tended to cloud my mood. The doctor who answered the original query about the poor unfortunate's distinctive pong put it down to a steroid compound. Lesser men might have queried the questioner's underwear.

It put me in mind of a woman I know who, although her personal daintiness could never be gainsaid, still gave off a marked whiff at close quarters. Body aromas may freely be discussed in the showers after a manly game of rugby or squash, but they're not the kind of subject that can be readily remarked upon over a rubber of ladies' bridge. Nevertheless one of my wife's pluckier friends took it upon herself to broach the unmentionable.

'Jane,' she said, 'what's that smell?'

'Lily of the valley,' came the reply. 'Do you like it?'

A woman of the shires of my acquaintance once told me of a trip to China as part of a group of Conservative ladies. As they gathered in the foyer of a Beijing hotel prior to an assault on the Great Wall, a group of Chinese women entered, all animated chatter. They stopped some yards away, sniffed, then turned as one and ran, choking, for the exits. The Conservative ladies put it down to their European perfumes, but it put a question mark over the whole day.

Then, in the same newspaper, another headline stopped me in my tracks: 'There's nothing more moral than *Big Brother*.' That's definitely not 'lily of the valley' . . .

8 January 2006

ASHES TO ASHES

A recent news item about how the numbers of people scattering the ashes of their dear departed on Britain's mountains was changing the nature of the soil on the peaks caused an understandable flicker of doubt among the thinking classes. We're not short of the odd mountain, so how many thousand grieving relatives scattering ash over hill and mountainside would it take to make the slightest difference to the soil there?

Apart from that, there's nature to contend with. A friend tells me that he has made three abortive attempts to scatter his granny's ashes on Ben Nevis, only to be repulsed by rain, wind and mist. It's all very well keeping to the old sailor's maxim of always spitting to the lee side, but the wind swirls around a bit on Nevis and he has no wish to be picking his relative's remains from between his teeth.

Another bereaved correspondent recounts the sad tale of his attempt to honour a much-loved old aunt's last wish to be spread over a particular garden of remembrance, only to be told that the garden was full. As his aunt had asked for that garden because all her best buddies were already there, he and his mother sneaked into the preferred garden and tipped the ashes furtively over the nearest bush. Out shot a hedgehog, covered in ash, and moving at a brisk pace. With a shriek, my correspondent's mother gave chase. She grabbed the unfortunate creature, rolled it in the grass, and then shook it vigorously in an attempt to restore the last of auntie to her desired resting place.

Then there's the Irish tale of the woman who kept her mother's ashes on the mantelpiece. Her husband, who had cared little for his mother-in-law in life, took to knocking the remains of his pipe into the urn. One day, a passing priest who had popped in for a drop of the hard stuff in his tea and had known the deceased well, lifted the urn's lid and peered at the ashes. 'D'you know, Mary,' he said, 'the mother's puttin' on weight.'

29 January 2006

GALLIC CHARM

Just when you think you have the measure of Johnny Foreigner . . .
We find ourselves in a farmyard, behind the church of a tiny
village, lost in the hills and woods of south-west France. This is the
place, we have been told, to buy brebis, the finest local cheese. An
attractive young Frenchwoman greets us.

'Brebis?' I say.

'Oui,' she replies with a smile. 'In the mountains.'

'In the mountains?' I ask, disappointed.

'Yes,' she replies, 'in the Pyrenees, with my husband.'

I can't believe it. I've spent half the day searching for this
place, and now she tells me the cheese is up a mountain miles
away. 'Can we order some?' I inquire.

'Oh, I don't know.'

My incredulity reaches new, hitherto unexplored limits. How
do these people stay in business? My wife intervenes. 'Le fromage,'
she says. 'Cheese.'

'Oh,' says the young woman, brightening. 'I thought you meant
the sheep. Of course you may buy the cheese.'

So could not someone have told me that brebis is a ewe as well
as a cheese?

Further hours of searching for the château reputed to produce
the best wine in the region bring us to a small broken sign; up a
narrow lane, through the vines, and the imposing house stands
before us. We ring the bell. An elderly woman's voice answers.
'We'd like to buy some wine.'

'Yes, what sort? Red, white, rosé?'

'Well, it depends . . .'

A sigh. 'Knock on the door on the left.'

I walk left, all the way around the great house, knocking

on every door I can find. No answer, not a saucisson. Then out of one door comes an elderly grump who, with no discernible enthusiasm, leads us into an office. With no encouragement we choose our wine. Grumpy produces an invoice, I produce a credit card. 'No cards,' he says.

I haven't a chequebook with me or enough cash. Back to the car, into town, find cash machine, back to the lost château. The wine is waiting for us, ready packed. 'I've given you a couple of extra bottles as a gift,' he says. I think I catch a glimpse of a smile . . . but I may have imagined it.

23 July 2006

OF COURSE WE BELIEVE YOU . . .

It has long been the contention of the thinking viewer that those in charge of television are convinced we're all eejits, a theory that recent programmes back to the hilt: an unfortunate wannabe gets dumped from one of these innumerable 'Search for a Star' epics. You know the sort of thing: 'You're going home . . . you are not Maria.' Exit hopeful, distraught, dreams in tatters, contemplating suicide.

Then, a week later, hallelujah! A surprise phone call to the loser's home. Can you believe it, it's the show's producer, they've had a rethink, and they're offering the broken hopeful another chance! What an incredible turn-up for the book; shocked surprise as our wannabe realises that all is not lost; cheers, tears, laughter – it's unbelievable!

It sure is, when you think that it has all been filmed, and the element of surprise may well have been dissipated or, at the very least, a question or two asked when the television camera crew turned up a couple of hours beforehand to capture the glorious moment.

Then there's the make-over show, where a gang of people build a new house in a week. The lucky family are 'surprised' at 7.30 in the morning by a huge television crew. All the family are up, scrubbed and dressed in their Sunday best. With hardly time to draw breath, not to mind pack, they're loaded into a car and sent off for a week's holiday. Never mind the luggage, what about work or school? And when the house is pulled down, gutted, what about the personal knick-knacks, the family heirlooms, the bits and pieces that every family gathers over the years?

Of course we believe you, we've only been watching television for the last fifty years. But boy, couldn't we all in real life do with builders who can arrive and finish on time? My daughter and her little family made the cardinal error of believing the builders when arranging to move lock, stock and barrel to their new home; it'll be at least three weeks from the due date before they can move in . . .

6 *August 2006*

NEW TRICKS

An eager viewer is enchanted with the new and exciting way of presenting television news, with the readers standing rather than sitting, particularly the BBC's Six O'Clock News, where endless variations have been added: firstly, the readers stand, then they sit, bringing it all to an exciting climax by standing again, before sitting down for the finish. Marvellous stuff! Creative broadcasting at its best – broadcasting that involves thought and flair, combined with pace and a frisson of the unexpected.

What a difference it would make if our radio newsreaders would get up and scamper about a bit, but the old ways die hard on the wireless. I asked a Radio 2 newsreader if he was standing or sitting. 'Lying down, actually,' he replied, a touch too languidly for my liking. And yet, radio news can provide moments television can only dream of. Last week, a Radio 4 announcer delivered himself of a flawless news story before pausing and saying: 'Ah! That was yesterday's bulletin, I'm afraid.'

As the long-suffering viewer will also testify, afternoons on ITV are a relentless barrage of ambulance-chasing lawyers, funeral expenses, dogs and elephants selling insurance, loans that will beggar your family for generations, stairlifts, walk-in baths, remedies for incontinence, diarrhoea and constipation, friendly bacteria, and varnish that does what it says on the tin. Could it be that ITV's decline might be due to factors other than its programmes?

Speaking of varnish, a listener recently painted a piece of wood, which she wished to put in water, so she carefully selected a tin of 'Yacht Varnish'. It was only when she had finished painting the boat that she read what it said on the tin: 'Not Suitable for Marine Use.'

13 August 2006

FORE!

The arrival of the American Ryder Cup team, clad in the kind of Glengarry tweed coats last worn by Edward VII while grouse-shooting, only added to my conviction that most Americans find anywhere outside of the Land of the Free and the Home of the Brave deeply confusing. Seeing them land at Dublin wearing Scottish tweed, reminded me of the country singer I met in Nashville who, when I told him that I came from Ireland, said: 'Oh, that's like Scotland, right?'

A further slap in the face to Ireland's pride was that the United States team brought with them their own supply of crisps. It's hardly calculated to lead to cordiality when you arrive in Ireland with your own potatoes . . .

Nobody goes to Ireland for the weather. The best times you'll have in the land of my fathers will be indoors, with a drop of whatever you're having yourself. So, while no one can doubt the warmth of the welcome, nor the impeccable state of the golf course, it was always on the cards that the Ryder Cup would be played in conditions that are referred to in Ireland as 'soft'. Once again, the Americans have exacerbated the situation: not content with bringing their own spuds, they've been followed by a hurricane.

As I write this, I know nothing of the upshot, and hope that the weather is clement; but if not, that somebody had the wit to call a halt in the wind and rain, and repair to a convenient hostelry. I can hear the hospitable Irish words from here: 'Will you be having another pint with your crisps, Tiger?' Crisps are called 'chips' in America, and what we know as chips used to be known there as 'french fries'. That was before Iraq. Now they're known as 'cheese-eating surrender-monkey fries' . . . To put the tin hat on it, a spy from the Emerald Isle tells me that in an attempt to enhance the country's reputation for green, green grass, which, like the shamrock, can only be found in Ireland, the fairways of the K Club, on which the Ryder Cup is being played, have been given a helping hand by being sprayed with green dye . . . Is there anything left in that bottle?

24 September 2006

IT'S ALL GO ROUND HERE

Around six o'clock on a misty autumn morning, I make my way along a quiet country road. Suddenly, another vehicle roars by at about 65 mph. As it sways from side to side, I see that it is no ordinary vehicle being driven insanely fast but a milk float, fully loaded. I've barely time to note that I'd no idea milk floats could go at that speed, when I'm passed by another tearaway.

This one is a police car, blue lights flashing, in hot pursuit of the milk float. I follow the high-speed chase along the deserted, narrow roads, until pursued and pursuer disappear down a one-track lane. It's the most exciting start to the day I've ever had, I feel as if I've taken part in a high-speed movie chase . . . What's the story behind such a bizarre occurrence? It can't be that the Boys in Blue were simply after a pinta, or that Express Dairies was living up to its name. My radio listeners' solutions were much more plausible: 'The fleeing milk float was obviously Sam, the herdsman from The Archers, distraught at Ruth's rejection of the previous night. The rascal has taken his revenge, left the Brookfield Farm milking parlour a smoking ruin, shut Bert in the tree house, and let the cows out onto the Grey Gables Golf Course . . .'

Feasible, but this seems more likely, from Ernie, The Fastest Milkman in The West: 'Thank you for getting out of the way this morning, as I was making my special delivery of fresh yoghurt to Highgrove. The police escort was to make sure I got there in time for HRH's breakfast.' Glad to be of service, sir.

12 November 2006

WHAT DO YOU THINK OF IT SO FAR?

This new money-saving wheeze of fortnightly rubbish collection has put the rat among the garbage, and no mistake. Even those of us who can scarcely remember what happened yesterday have a vague folk memory that last week, residents were being fined for putting out their rubbish a few hours early, on the grounds of health, safety and vermin. And you can store rubbish for two weeks without causing even worse problems?

Still, never mind, as long as you're doing your bit to save the planet by recycling. The artist Tim Gustard tells me of his framer, who decided to have a big clear-out of his workshop. He filled his car with wooden frames and cardboard and took it off to the brand-new, highly expensive recycling unit. He didn't get through the gate.

'You can't bring that in 'ere mate.'

'Why not?'

'Business rubbish.'

'So, what do you suggest I do with it?'

'Not my problem, mate'.

After a terse exchange, the framer returned home and rang his local (Eden) district council. They apologised for their employee's attitude, and told our man that he could purchase bags and stickers and put the rubbish out for weekly collection. Further, he could put out as much as he liked, and it would only cost a pound a week.

Result! A pound a week, cheaper than the cost of driving to the tip, and more environmentally friendly.

'And will it be recycled?' he asked the man from the council.

'Oh no, sir, it will go for landfill with the rest of the rubbish.'

A listener was delighted to learn how his efforts at recycling were helping to offset global warming. His local council sent a circular to explain how certain items were recycled. For instance, plastic milk cartons are sent by road from Sussex to Bolton in Lancashire, where they're packaged, sent on to the docks, to then travel 6,000 miles by container ship to China, where they are smartly turned into plastic garden furniture, and shipped back in containers to us. That's a carbon footprint and a half.

It gave my listener pause, and caused him to check how many of his household products originated in the Orient: garden chairs, of course, radio, alarm clock, hand cream, telephone, drinking mug, books. A relief to know that the Chinese take-away he ordered was made in Britain . . .

29 April 2007

GIMME SHELTER

News that an EU directive is going to force equal rights for women upon golf and working men's clubs predictably brought the curmudgeons out from behind the wainscoting: 'Does this mean that we men can have fluffy towels and perfumed soap in our showers, two courtesy shots in pro-ams, play from the front tees, and have our fees reduced?' 'Why do women want to join a club where they are not wanted? Why not set up their own club, and ban the men?' 'Will I have to part with my titanium driver and go back to my old hickory-shaft so as not to gain an unfair advantage?' 'Will gimmees become longer?' This latter query shows lamentable ignorance of the niceties of women's golf; for there are no 'gimmees' (conceded short putts) in the ladies' game. 'Let's see that one in,' is the watchword.

Then there was the predictable, 'If women get equal rights on the golf course and the freedom to breastfeed in public, will this not interfere with their swing?' Gentlemen, gentlemen.

Meanwhile, a friend wonders if the boffins aren't missing something: very soon all public places will be smoke-free. But, to get to a public place, you have to pass through its entrance, where you find groups of people puffing away like things possessed. Is passing through a smokescreen to get to a smoke-free zone good for you? Ireland has been 'smoke-free' for a couple of years now, and apart from the odd smoker being sent flying by a passing bus as he has a drag on the road outside the pub, the effect has been beneficial. My own experience last year, as I attended a grand function in a Dublin hotel ballroom, was that just after the coffee was served to the several hundred people there, the great room emptied as if by magic. The present Lady Wogan and I took the hint and left as well, only to find all our fellow diners standing in the car park in the rain . . . smoking.

17 June 2007

GREEN-SKY THINKING

A listener, browsing through the tangled undergrowth of the BBC website, with its tales of terrorism, global warming and the race to build another Noah's Ark, came across the story of a new aeroplane. At the beginning of the report, the BBC put its most important question to us all: 'Boeing unveils a new jet, the only big commercial aircraft made more of carbon fibre than aluminium. But is it more environmentally friendly?'

Is it environmentally friendly? For heaven's sake! Is it safe? That's the important question. Then, how many hours to get on and off? Get through security? And how many days before your luggage appears in the baggage hall? Remember that eejit who said that the biggest threat to us all was not terrorism, but global warming? Is there a hope in hell that we're ever going to get our priorities right?

As concerned, environmentally friendly folk, we're all too aware of the need to protect the planet, but when there are more and more gas-guzzlers and lorries than ever on the road, more planes, more people, is it really necessary to confine cows and sheep for long periods, in order to measure the effect their flatulence is having on the ozone layer? Mark my words, the days of the baked bean are numbered.

While not wishing to pursue what advertisers call 'trapped wind' (surely a misnomer, it's the 'escaped wind' that gives the trouble), I was interested to hear a vegetarian claim superior status to the meat-eater in the carbon footprint game, on the grounds that they didn't eat cattle or sheep. Then a further proposition, that, like worthy married couples, veggie-eaters should get £20 a week for not eating meat and therefore not contributing to the 250 litres a day of methane each animal emits.

A spurious claim when one thinks of the damage that can be

done by the aforementioned bean. And think of the consequences in a confined space that can be caused by leeks, cabbage and sprouts, to name but a few. The saintly Attenborough himself will bear witness to the constant eruptions of herbivores such as mountain gorillas. It's not the meat-eaters, it's the meat.

15 July 2007

KEEPING UP WITH THE JONESES

A listener, obviously at the end of his tether, notes that council tax revaluers want to charge us more if we live in a 'nice' area, which surely ought to mean discounts for those of us who live in a 'rough' area, as this unfortunate obviously does: 'We have a huge council house in our street. The extended family is run by a woman with a pack of dogs. Her car isn't taxed or insured; it doesn't even have a number plate, but the police do nothing about it. Her grumpy old man is famous for upsetting foreigners with racist comments. A local shopkeeper blames him for ordering the murder of his son's girlfriend, but nothing has been proved. Two of the kids have broken marriages, and two grandsons are meant to be in the Army, but are always out at nightclubs. The family's odd antics are forever in the papers. They're out of control. Who'd want to live near Windsor Castle?'

Meanwhile, Elfin Safety continues to bemuse: an elderly gentleman, upon leaving hospital, was issued with a stool on which to rest a sore leg. The little stool carried a warning: 'Do not attempt to use this until the clinician has demonstrated the correct method.' The old man's family took a chance, and stood the stool upright on its legs. Let's hope they don't regret such a foolhardy action.

Recently, a friend's mother-in-law, aged 91, fell and broke her pelvis, which caused her a few problems . . . one of which was the arrival of the regulation free-gift commode. She was cheered enormously by the warning: 'This item is not intended to be used as a seat and should not be used before being demonstrated by a trained health professional.' Now, that's a job and a half . . . imagine the strain of demonstrating half a dozen of those a day.

14 October 2007

WEIGHTY MATTERS

It can't be easy to keep the populace in a permanent state of near-panic, but this Government certainly tries. Not a week goes by but we are threatened by some new pestilence or disaster: avian flu, foot and mouth, bluetongue, booze, stressed toddlers, climate change, terrorism and, according to Health Secretary Alan Johnson, most dangerous of all, obesity. 'A greater threat than global warming,' says Al. Hang on, wasn't it only last year that we were warned that global warming was a greater threat than terrorism? Which can only mean that obesity is a greater threat than terrorism. A shrewd listener has the answer: scrap the ID cards idea and bring in food rationing instead.

So, how can an increased number of fat people threaten all life on the planet? Another listener of mine speculates that it may well be that heavier people have a deeper carbon footprint, and the weight of all those fat people might easily break through the earth's crust, causing earthquakes, destroying life as we know it: perhaps the increase in weight will cause the earth to alter orbit. Or is it just the nameless dread that fat people are going to gobble up all the food?

Thank goodness 'research shows' that it's not our fault, but the result 'of a society in which energy-dense and cheap foods, labour-saving devices, motorised transport and sedentary work are rife'. The obvious conclusion is that speeding drivers can't be blamed, because modern cars have the ability to go too fast, and murderers are not at fault because somebody invented guns and knives . . .

Who's going to carry the can then? Well, we are told by those in high office that by 2040, most of the next generation will be obese, due not just to Turkey Twizzlers but lack of exercise.

Just refresh my memory: who has been responsible for selling off school playgrounds and playing fields over the past 10 years? Who was it decided that competition was bad for kids, as there would be losers, so sports days were cancelled? And who was it that allowed those in charge to be sued if anyone grazed their knees, or barked their knuckles playing conkers?

Some people, of course, will never get the message: 'It was good to hear the news that if I make myself obese, I stand a 50/50 chance of living until 2040.'

21 October 2007

ONCE MORE UNTO THE BREACH . . .

How many hallelujahs Gordon and Harriet must have offered up on behalf of dear Harry Redknapp, for taking off at least some of the pressure of this, their 'semanus horribilis'. If the fellow isn't in line for a gong in the New Year's Honours List on the strength of it, I'll be amazed, and he must now be the front runner for the vacant England football managership . . . though why anybody would want to touch that poisoned chalice of a job with a corner flag is beyond me.

From Walter Winterbottom through Alf Ramsey, on to Keegan, Taylor, Eriksson and the latest corpse, McClaren, the job has been a recipe for rejection, scorn, insult and, ultimately, a nation's revulsion. You take the job trailing clouds of glory, and you inevitably end up shot from the skies like a rocketing pheasant. No other job carries such a taint, such pitiful certainty of abasement on a national scale . . . Apart from one other. Oh, Gordon, and you wanted it so badly.

Since no football manager in their right mind will take the England job, it has been suggested to me by more than one 'resting' thespian that it might with profit be offered to an actor-manager . . .

Even as we speak, there are men slumbering in the armchairs of the Garrick, the Arts, yes, even the Groucho, who would spring to their feet with cries of 'That should be me, up there!', at such an offer. Their services would be cheaply and readily bought with a small bundle of crisp white fivers in a plain brown envelope. What a boon such a man would be to England's under-motivated lads. Tales of Larry and Johnny would set them in a roar on the practice ground, promoting the spirit of easy bonhomie so sadly lacking since 1966.

At the actor-manager's request, great names of the theatre

would readily turn up on match days to inspire and motivate the lads. Think of the effect a gentle word or two from Dame Judi would have. Or Sir Donald Sinden, intoning Henry's great speech at Agincourt, just before the team take to the field! There's a risk that it might end badly, of course, with the penalty area covered up with our English dead, but I'll tell you this, love . . . Johnny Foreigner would know that he'd been in a fight.

2 December 2007

WISDOM OF THE AGES

A London taxi driver writes: 'Ere. D'you know who I had in the back of my cab last week? Bloke from the BBC. I says, "What's all this stuff about you lot telling people to phone up if they've been affected by the programmes? You don't wanna do that . . . just say, if you've been affected by any issues in this programme, you need to stop watching the telly. It's not real, it's just acting. Get out a bit more . . ." When I turned around, he'd gone.'

A day or two later, my taxi-driving correspondent wrote again: 'Ere. Guess who I had in the back of my cab yesterday. This geezer who says that these high-pitched sound devices being used by the police to disperse gangs of yoofs should be scrapped. "I agree!" I says. "Whatever happened to the good old baton charge?" Well, he seemed like my sort of bloke, but he never left a tip.'

A 'Saunders of Bungay' speculates correctly on a considerable amount of concerned reaction, mainly in green ink, about the rights of yoof not to be discomfited by these 'mosquito' (there's original) devices emitting a high-pitched noise. His concern is more prosaic: there must be places run by the young who could easily do the same to old fogies who they wanted to take a powder. He thinks a picture of Graham Norton would do it for most people, or the sound of Ken Livingstone.

The trouble is, those well-stricken in years are proof against anything they cannot hear, or are wearing their wives' glasses. Saunders espouses a weapon that would straddle the age gap, and frighten the sturdiest horse. For example, his wife has proposed a public showing of a home movie of his daughter's wedding, featuring Saunders telling an off-colour joke, and doing the twist. She says she's sure that it would clear Manchester, not just a parade of shops.

A member of the Armed Forces has written to me on the

vexed topic of yoof, in typically trenchant terms. He suggests the following rallying cry: 'Teenagers! Tired of being harassed by your stupid parents? Act now! Move out, get a job, pay your own bills! Do it, while you still know everything.'

17 February 2008

SKIN DEEP

Perhaps it was the sainted Delia opening a tin of custard, but I happened to mention on the radio that although my mother 'couldn't boil water', there was little she could do to destroy a custard straight from the tin, and I took particular delight in the 'skin' on the top of the bowl. Rarely have I struck such a responsive chord in the hearts of the Great British Public. The consensus was that there couldn't be much wrong with a man of such discerning taste, and that I should run for public office. My producer, Barrowlands Boyd, took the gastronomic motif a stage further by rhapsodising on the 'skin' of rice pudding. This really brought them out from behind the skirting board.

Of the heaving postbag, I offer a listener who told of his late father, who persuaded Mum to make the custard in a bowl three times as wide as it was high, thus achieving the perfect ratio of skin to custard, and sparing the family the unpleasantness of the usual bout of fisticuffs between his father and himself. In the case of the rice pudding, the ratio was extended to at least six times as wide as the depth of pud. My listener went further, with the culinary hint that, like Tony Hancock's mother's gravy, the skin of the pud should gently undulate, under a crisp, brown texture. It's a cry from the heart from a public pushed to the limit by Jennie Bond and 'Great British Chefs' which last week brought us 'Rhubarb infused with tobacco, Chicken Popcorn, and Confit of Coxcomb'.

The way things are going, we'll be lucky to have anything to eat, with prices rocketing and the starving rioting. This is because land has to be turned over to produce bio-fuels, so that we won't get burnt to a crisp by global warming through use of fossil fuels. Sorry, but Brussels insists. This is leading to the cutting-down of vast swathes of forests. Yes, the same forests that used to absorb the carbon that is warming the planet. Do you ever feel that we're going around in circles ?

20 April 2008

SURELY YOU'RE CHOKING?

A teacher writes of a recent first aid training day at her school. It was not as straightforward as you may think, since the dreaded Health and Safety cast its dark shadow over all common sense. Just in case it ever comes up, if you see someone choking (even if it's someone you know) you have to ask first, 'Are you choking?' Then you may only administer the first aid if they say, or more likely, nod, their agreement. Otherwise, technically, they may sue you for assault. You must not refer to the 'Heimlich manoeuvre' (a process where you squeeze the choker from behind, to expel the obstruction) but say 'abdominal thrusts' or pay copyright to Mr Heimlich.

There's more: if a child has suffered a scrape or cut, teachers may not stick on a plaster themselves, but offer it for inspection, in the hope that the plaster ends up covering the wound – tricky enough, if the wound is not visible to the child. One example: when a boy sustained an injury to his back, his parents were telephoned but were unable to go to assist. Blind panic, until somebody remembered that the lad had a brother in the school. He was rushed to the scene so that he could lift his brother's shirt for inspection. You see, touching a child's clothing is not allowed . . .

Further tales from the Health and Safety Handbook for the Demented: a Mr Allrite (nobody writes to me under their real name) says that he bought a small padlock for his shed. The instructions read: 'Please ensure that appropriate personal protection equipment (PPE) is worn while using this product.' Carefully deciphering the little pictures on the packet, he purchased a face mask, ear defenders, safety glasses and protective gloves. Then, new padlock in glove, breathless under the mask, glasses steamed up, and rendered deaf by the ear defenders, he tripped on the shed step and suffered serious contusions to his head. He wonders if he should get in touch with Injury Lawyers For You about the lack of a picture of a hard hat on the packaging.

27 April 2008

SPIT AND POLISH

Speaking to my friend Peter Alliss recently, I remarked to the Grand Old Man of Golf how, while watching the recent Masters championship on television, many a delicately nurtured follower of the great game had been taken aback to see the peerless Tiger Woods spitting freely about the green sward. Ever conscious of the sensibilities of his audience, Peter told me that he had taken up this very point with American commentators and, to a man, they simply didn't understand what he was complaining about. Spitting, it turns out, is simply part and parcel of the American Way, particularly in the sports arena. You're nothing if you don't let fly with a manly expectoration on the pitcher's mound at baseball. We're well used to it here at every televised football match, where the spitting appears to be as competitive as the game itself.

Strangely enough, I've never seen a player spit on the rugby field, apart from blood, but spitting on the course at the gentleman's game of golf? It'll be the Centre Court at Wimbledon next. Oh, Tim's already done it? Then, a passing listener explained the reason for the British reserve with regard to the phlegm. In the early part of the last century, when TB was rampant, it was thought that the disease was spread by spitting. So parlous was the situation that the government of the day passed a law against it, with a heavy fine imposed on the careless spitter.

My informant was hesitant about bringing this up, what with the present Government's inclination to tax and fine everyone and everything that moves. With the public's proclivity to spit for fun, Gordon and Alistair could have a field day. On the other hand, with the tax raised, Gordon might be able to buy back our gold, repeal the 10p thing and give everyone back their pensions. I'd commend the idea to the House, if I thought anybody cared.

4 May 2008

CHECKING OUT

If my postbag is anything to go by, there is nothing that gets up the collective nose of those, like myself, in the prime of life more than Health and Safety, and particularly its spotty-faced offspring at supermarket checkouts. I know you'll say, ever fair-minded, that it's not their fault, they're only following orders, but I'm sorry, that excuse didn't wash with the Nazis during the last unpleasantness and it doesn't cut the mustard with my crowd these days, either.

It's the ageist slur that cuts to the quick . . . A lady arrives at the check-out with a couple of bottles of wine. She is 66 years of age. 'Are you over 18?' A 36-year-old woman arrives at the checkout with a lobster, fresh scallops and a bottle of gin. Same question from the girl at the till. Unfortunately, the customer was unable to produce a utilities bill in her name, or a parchment driving licence, and had to abandon her gin. She idly wondered if the average 17-year-old's booze of choice was a bottle of gin to wash down their crustacea.

Percy, 58 and a non-drinker, tried to purchase some bottles of non-alcoholic wine and beer, and was asked his age at the checkout. He pointed out that the stuff was non-alcoholic. He was sharply told that the words 'wine' and 'beer' featured on the bottles, and kindly produce some identification, or else. It was else, he hadn't got his papers. Then there's Nick, fully accredited, thank goodness, at a youthful 60, waiting 10 minutes at the checkout for a supervisor to arrive, because the girl is under 21 and needs permission to put the booze through. It not just the demon drink either: a 55-year-old woman, subjected to interrogation for a pair of kitchen scissors, a 27-year-old trying to buy some spoons for the office, asked for identification as you had to be over 16 to buy cutlery.

We could look on the bright side, of course, and take it as an immense compliment that, although well stricken in years, we still carry the bloom of youth. As a hurt 55-year-old wrote: 'There are worse things than being asked if you're over 18. Not being asked.' Now we all appreciate that in the current parlous climate of knife crime and youthful binge drinking, supermarkets must exercise due caution; but can people not be encouraged to use their eyes, judgement and even common sense? Sorry, even as I wrote that, I knew it was silly . . .

27 July 2008

CAUSE AND EFFECT

You can't beat a think-tank for getting up the public's nose. Apparently, of all the nations of the known world, the Brits are the least likely to have a go at the wrongdoer, eschewing the valorous citizen's arrest in favour of discretion, and preferring to leave it to the forces of law and order, and, in the likely event of the absence of the boys in blue, hurriedly crossing to the other side of the street. My listeners were quick to the ramparts, pointing out that we are forever being told by the police not to get involved, and if you do, and you're not stabbed, shot or had your head kicked in, you're the one likely to be arrested, particularly if you got your retaliation in first by, say, tapping the miscreant on the head with a feather duster. According to my crowd, your rozzer likes nothing better than an easy collar, and while the culprit is legging it, the proud defender of his hearth and home will find himself in the slammer for not having a light over his rear number plate.

Barely had the dust settled before parents were being advised how best to spot criminal tendencies in their kiddies. Once more unto the breach: who are the biggest fools? Those handing out these idiotic mandates, or us, for paying these numpties to sit in Parliament and come up with such tosh. Wouldn't it be better to issue 'Parent Packs', with callipers and measuring tape to check the circumference of the children's heads, the distance between the eyes, etc. 'Eugenics', the new buzzword this autumn. So, parents are advised that if they suspect that their children are in a gang, because they inexplicably have money, they are advised to 'tell a youth group'. And crime has worsened because of British citizens abdicating responsibility. Anyone spot the missing link?

7 September 2008

THE WHISTLE OF THE ONCOMING TRAIN

At the risk of flogging the dead horse . . . Not by the merest flicker of an eyelash has Alistair Darling allowed us as much as a glimpse into his inner turmoil over the current financial unpleasantness. I suspect he has been tutored in this by old Golden Brown, master of the inscrutable countenance. 'Preserve the appearance and demeanour of the cigar-store Indian, Ali,' the PM would have counselled in his warm, persuasive Scots burr. 'Never let the buggers know what you're thinking.' Wrong! A chancellor of the old school, hiding behind his pince-nez, wing collar and homburg hat, might have got away with tight lips and a swish of his tailcoat, but not today, Al. We know all too well that the banks, stock markets and world economies are up to their armpits in the slurry, and we have all been dragged in there with them. So, for everybody's sake, and your own sanity Al, let it out. You could do worse than take a leaf from X Factor contenders' books and, sobbing uncontrollably, tell us how your 'journey' has ended in disappointment and broken dreams.

You may well ask how it is that, in a financial world heaving with experts, analysts and gurus, nobody heard the whistle of the oncoming train. Ah, but one did. One shrewd observer looked into the future and got out while the going was good. Wherever he is, I fancy I can hear the faint echo of his laughter from here. Timing. It's a gift, isn't it, Tone? Don't you think so, Gordon?

A friend of mine is thinking of buying shares in Robert Peston, the BBC's Business Editor. While all around him are falling like ninepins, he's all over the television like a cheap suit. Huw and Fiona must be sick of the sight of him; he's probably demanding a clothes allowance and his own wardrobe lady, even as we speak. His every comment causes a fit in the City, his 'blog' has bank shares rising and falling like bees' wings. The man has the country's fate in his hands. Do you think he could tell us who's going to be next to get the push from *Strictly Come Dancing*?

A final thought from one not versed in the arcane ways of high finance: rather than the Government lending the taxpayers' money to the banks, why not let the taxpayer keep the money, leave it in the bank, and cut out the middleman?

12 October 2008

A PICTURE SPEAKS A
THOUSAND WORDS . . . ?

We've only speculated on the possibility before now, but there can be little doubt, following a chaotic couple of weeks, that television news editors think that the rest of us are a bunch of numpties. Consider the other weekend, with a serious-faced reporter doing his pieces on the key players in the financial unpleasantness. To facilitate the childlike understanding of eejits like you and me, the visual aid was fish. Thus, big fish and little fish, all caught up in the net. To illustrate, our newshound shrewdly positioned himself at a wet-fish shop. When he mentioned a 'big fish', he picked up a salmon from the slab, and when a 'small fish', he picked up a mackerel.

A correspondent found this splendidly enlightening as, until he had seen this item, he'd often wondered just how big and small players in the global money market differed. He said the scales fell from his eyes . . .

The combination of newsreader Huw Edwards and Economics editor Hugh Pym is lightening the gloom of the BBC News at Ten.
  'Over to you, Hugh.'
  'Thank you, Huw . . . Back to you, Huw.'
  'Thank you, Hugh.'
Hugh is enthusiastically carrying on the tradition of helping us understand complex economic issues by assuming the viewer's mental age to be about seven. Last year, you may remember, the previous editor, Evan Davis, illustrating an 'economic crossroads' by standing, you've guessed it, at a wet and windy rural crossroads. The other day, Mr Pym helped us understand the concept

of inflation going up and down by standing inside a lift going, yes, up and down.

Then, there was the 'domino effect' on the 'real economy', colourfully pictured for our numbed brains by a stack of upended dominoes falling backwards. And last week Hugh put the tin hat on it by demonstrating the need for 'increased liquidity' in the money markets, with, you've got it in one, an overflowing pint glass of water. Well, I never.

For what it's worth, I pass on a thrifty tip for the ladies from a listener of mine, Tina of Hornchurch, where good husbandry is the watchword. 'Ladies, not sure where to put your money these days? Save pounds by padding your bras with your cash. It will keep the chest warm for the winter, and you'll find that it generates quite a bit of interest.'

26 October 2008

MERRY CHRISTMAS, ONE AND ALL

As with Democracy, the price of Health and Safety is eternal vigilance, and examples of local councils' insane strictures roll in . . . A town's traditional Christmas tree, coming from sustainable forestry, and recyclable, has been abandoned in favour of a plastic one – on environmental grounds. Guides and Brownies in another bewildered location have been prevented from singing carols in a local shopping centre, in case people stop and listen, and cause other shoppers to trip over them. Church bell-ringers have been told to wear earmuffs and protective helmets – bats in the belfry. The congregation of another church recently found that all the hassocks had disappeared. The vicar had been advised by Health and Safety that the church would be held responsible if anyone tripped over or fell off a hassock. How high are your church's hassocks? And a council has just received orders from the highest level not to use the phrase 'Singing from the same hymn sheet', for fear of upsetting atheists. It's Hell out there, even for those who don't believe in it.

Like the rest of us, my friend Saunders (of Bungay, not the River) spent a dilettante's weekend ploughing through endless tosh, recycled by newspapers every Christmas, on 'How to survive the office party', 'How to cure a hangover', 'How to cook the turkey, 'Who's got the best crackers/cakes/puddings', 'Revolting cocktails' and 'Cheap plonk that will kill the taste of mum's sprouts'. This shrewd if world-weary observer claims never to read any useful stuff on how to survive the Festive Season and offers his own tips on how to come out the other side. 1) Office parties are only a ploy to cheapen you, and afford lesser employees a chance to step into your shoes. Make some plausible excuse (a vigil for the homeless at Christmas, perhaps), and Don't Go! 2) There is no known cure for a hangover, apart from steady drinking. Take the pledge. You'll see everybody in a different light, and leave home for ever on Boxing Day. 3) The first rule of Christmas is that the benighted turkey will be either cremated or undercooked. Buy a large chicken, stuff it with popcorn, and when it blasts its way out of the oven, it's done.

And finally . . . a most useful suggestion for a stress-free Christmas: stuff the turkey with Prozac.

7 December 2008

FAME AND FORTUNE

Whenever I turn on the television these days, I see young people degrading themselves in the pursuit of fame and, what's worse, older folk attempting to rekindle the flame of fame by similar degradation in the Big House, Jungle or Kitchen. If only they knew . . .

Last week, at a Christmas party, a distinguished-looking woman gave me more than a passing glance. I responded, as any gentleman would, with a winsome smile. She came over to me. 'Do I know you?' she said. I told her my name. A faint glimmer of recognition crept over her fine features. 'Ah,' she said, 'I don't watch the television, apart from the news.' She then went on to lament the fate of Ed Stourton, with a passing reference to Jonathan Ross, whom she claimed never to have seen, but had read about. Like most who claim 'never to watch television', had we continued our discourse she would doubtless have expressed forthright opinions on *Strictly* . . . and *The X Factor*, but a tide of lunch-seekers swept us apart. Those 'a cut above' seem to watch popular television by accident or osmosis.

It's been my experience that a well-known face is not all that it's cracked up to be, and my theory, yet to be exploded, that the public think that everybody who appears on television is freely interchangeable is backed up by the hard fact that for years, Parkinson, Aspel, Harty and I were thought to be one and the same. People would sympathise with me for Oliver Reed's appalling behaviour (Aspel), Rod Hull's Emu attempting to strangle me (Parkinson) or Grace Jones giving me a right-hander across the chops (Harty). For years, when I first arrived from Erin's Isle, people never knew the difference between Eamonn Andrews, Val Doonican and myself. I first found that cruel mistress, Fame, when but a boy broadcaster in Ireland. Within months, I found that I could no longer frequent my favourite pub without someone either fawning over me or inviting me outside for a bout of fisticuffs. Whereas in the past I could walk down O'Connell Street without a Grecian bend, now I had old biddies calling after me: 'Terry Wogan. Thinks he's ******* gorgeous!' I thought it would be different in Britain, more reserved, until stopped in Carnaby Street by a gent who said, 'Here! Sign this, would you? It's for my wife. I can't stand you myself.' Fame . . . Footprints on the sands of time? I don't think so.

28 December 2008

BUMPING INTO THE FURNITURE

Comment on the new light bulbs being foisted upon us in the sacred name of the environment is now superfluous. We must cheerfully accept the fact that in the future, we will spend much of our time in the gloaming, bumping into the furniture and reading only in the daytime. Useless to point to the huge office buildings and unfinished structures ablaze with light, as we travel into London and every other city every morning, knowing full well that those lights have been on all night. As long as we're doing our bit . . . Like the many who obeyed environmental entreaties to replace their boilers with 'highly efficient' Grade A condensing boilers – £ 3,000 later, they're spending time wrapping their outlet pipes in hot-water bottles and blankets. It appears that these super-efficient boilers don't like the cold. Any more than the fridge-freezer bought last October by a listener. At the beginning of December, it defrosted. The engineer pursed his lips, sucked in air between his teeth, and said that the kitchen wasn't warm enough: it needed to be at a steady temperature of 10°C (50°F) for the fridge-freezer to keep working. So, fridge-freezers don't like the cold weather, either . . .

Still, the chill is a talking point when conversation flags in the snug; just let's not get carried away. It's been cold, but not, as the TV weather boys and girls persist in describing it, 'bitterly' cold. Even at −10°C (14°F), we don't do 'bitterly'. In Manitoba, Canada, a few days ago, it was −35°C (−31°F), with a wind-chill factor of −50°C. That's bitter, and you know, people there got on with their lives. And I'll bet their boilers didn't burst.

Another listener lives on the side of a steep hill and, after the snow flurries and hard frosts of earlier in the week, clapped her mittened hands with glee to see the gritting lorry arrive to do its worthy work. Well done, the local council. Picture then her surprise, with further snow and ice predicted, to see, on the following morning, a council road-sweeping lorry meticulously sweeping away all the said salty grit. Elsewhere, householders were informed that there would be no refuse collection for at least a week. 'Refuse collectors sustained injuries in the icy conditions, and collections have been cancelled.' What next? Too wet and windy in March and April? Risk of sunburn in summer? Leaves making it risky underfoot in autumn? And you have the nerve to complain about your council tax?

11 January 2009

MYTHS AND LEGENDS

What brought it on was a cleaner walking into my radio studio the other morning to empty the waste-paper basket. Fair enough, one woman, one job, I hear you cry. Except that I was on the air, broadcasting to the dozing millions at the time. Proof, if proof were needed, of what I had long suspected: the cleaners in BBC Radio 2, Western House, don't know that they're working in a radio station. Most, I'm sure, exchange cheery banter on the strange nature, and even stranger inhabitants, of the office block in which they find themselves working. I imagine them remarking on the ever-present elevator music and the solitary figures hunched over twinkling desks, talking to themselves.

I shared with my listeners my pleasure in my unexpected visitor, and of course they had to top it. The first, a tale from Spain, of an intensive care unit there where staff were perplexed, and then panicked, by the death of a patient at 10.30 a.m. on a Tuesday – every Tuesday, at exactly the same time, week after week. After a far-reaching inquiry, the tragic solution came to light. Every Tuesday at 10.30, the cleaner would remove a plug in order to vacuum the ward floor, thus fatally rendering useless a life-support system. No sooner had I recounted this sad, if hysterical, tale than I was subjected to a barrage of contumely from smart alecks, who claimed to have heard it all before, in various guises, and took exception to my recycling a 'tired old urban myth'. Tchah! Crocodiles in sewers, that's an urban myth.

My cough was softened by a former banker, a decent soul whose early years, like my own, were marked by the constant sorting of half-crowns from two-bob bits. He recalled working in a bank that had one of the then new-fangled ATMs installed. A boon to the weary teller, and the manager's pride and joy. Except that every morning at 11.30 the thing gave a gasp and expired, leading to schism and doubt among the customers. Once again a rigorous inquiry was initiated. IT experts were called in. It took a couple of days before it transpired that the manager's secretary was unplugging the machine so that she could plug in the kettle for the old boy's morning tea.

I fully realise that nobody under 35 will believe that story either, never having actually seen a bank manager.

22 February 2009

DEEP WATERS

A long time ago, I sat an examination for a banking qualification. While I only passed the intermediate test before the siren call of the circus led me to the gypsy existence in which you currently find me, the public have been lured into the false supposition that I am some kind of financial guru.

My phantom banking qualification is one which others in charge of our current parlous financial situation, such as the Chancellor, the Prime Minister and Fred Goodwin, among others, also seem to lack. (Alistair, a word of advice: debit the receiver, credit the giver, and you'll not go far wrong.)

Regardless, I have been bombarded with comments on the present economic crisis from members of the public. Having read their views, I'll only say that any government which thinks that it is fooling us with fiscal flummery is sorely mistaken. The public can see the blindingly obvious when it's in front of them.

'For some months,' begins one missive, 'we've been hearing that, since our privately owned banks have got into trouble, the only way for the Government to save them is to buy a big slice of the banks and put it into public ownership. And now, since the publicly owned Post Office has run into difficulties, the only way it can be saved from rack and ruin is to sell off a big slice and put it into private ownership. Anyone spot the deliberate error there?'

Then came this brief but pointed list of 'truths for today': 'rewarding failure will reduce the number of failures,' it read. 'Punishing success will encourage more success. You can get out of debt by going further into debt. The best people to get you out of trouble are the people who put you in it in the first place.'

However, nothing provoked a bigger reaction this week than the story of the mother refused entry to a swimming pool because she had two children with her, and the new Health and Safety rule stipulates 'one child, one adult'. The fact that one child held three swimming certificates cut no ice with the jobsworth on the turnstile.

So the mother shrewdly solved the problem by taking along her 76-year-old father-in-law, who is terrified of water and unable to swim. That's OK! Come in, the water's fine . . .

1 March 2009

INTERNATIONAL RELATIONS

The other week, at the invitation of the European Broadcasting Union and its director, Björn Erichsen, I delivered the keynote speech on Common Focus Day to the delegates gathered together for the Golden Rose awards, and the EBU's annual conference in Lucerne. Mr Erichsen accused me last year of undermining the Eurovision Song Contest by my less-than-respectful commentaries over the years, but no hard feelings, I was honoured to be invited to address such a distinguished gathering of the cream of European television. 'In heaven's name, why pick a numpty like you?' I hear you cry . . . Well, I always suspected as much, but having met the people who run the EBU, and therefore the Eurovision, they don't think we take it seriously enough. They think that the British attitude to the old Eurosong is reflective of what they perceive to be our attitude to Europe: our hearts are not in it. We don't give it enough respect, and it's MY fault.

So, who better to explain myself, and the UK's less-than-serious attitude to the Great Contest? I tried to assuage Mr Erichsen's annoyance at our cavalier stance, despite the fact that the contest commands one of the UK's biggest television audiences of the year, by assuring him and the 750 delegates that Britain loves the Eurovision, and nobody more than me; why else would I have been there every year since the Peninsular War? I told them that my approach was that true friends do not indulge in flattery or sycophancy, but in good-natured banter. If a friend does something silly, you tell him so, and he'll do the same for you. The Eurovision is a magnificent concept, the coming-together of the nations on wings of song, but it's not a war. It's light entertainment, a technical tour de force.

I said that I detected a certain disenchantment among the British public, and pointed out that the UK public vote has always been for their choice of the best song, whether Russian, Croatian, Albanian or even French. It offends our sense of fair play to see blatant voting for allies and neighbours, even in the context of something so light-hearted and, occasionally, deeply silly.

The body of the hall rose to me, and later the Director General told me that I had converted him. Wogan and Britain vindicated.

Then a supposedly reputable newspaper that specialises in 'Meeja' comes up the following day with the headline, 'Wogan says Eurovision is rubbish'.

I give up . . .

17 May 2009

DON'T PANIC!

'Wass' goin' on?' a phrase, we are assured by the producer, which is no longer acceptable on EastEnders, but which was my immediate reaction on returning to Blighty's blighted shores last week. I turn my back for five minutes, and, as Yeats put it, 'All is changed, changed utterly'. For a start, what happened to swine flu? When I left a couple of weeks ago, people were going down like flies; anybody who'd ever been to Mexico was hurled into a darkened room, and the key thrown away, dire warnings of universal sickness were issuing from the World Health Organisation every hour, on the hour. The force of it all struck home at Rome airport where I saw two Americans (it would be, wouldn't it?) sitting in the lounge fully masked up against any passing bug. I only know that they were Americans because the man took his mask off to order a drink, and to eat. Maybe he thought that the swine flu wouldn't attack anybody with their mouth full . . . So I get back, preparing to step over the dead and the dying, and stone me, it's all gone.

Just like mad cow disease and avian flu, without so much as a 'by your leave', and not a word from the harbingers of doom, the WHO (and was ever an organisation better named?). So, where did it go? Back to the unfortunate swine of Mexico? It worries me that one dreadful day some real and terrible pestilence is going to come out of nowhere, and we'll be so fed up with the crying of 'Wolf!' from the authorities that we'll pay no attention, and get it in the neck.

The lack of any distracting scare over the past couple of weeks has meant that the public eye is back on the ball, with disastrous results for the Government. Picture the scene in Cabinet:

'We've got to get them worried about something else, or we're finished!'

'Yes, Prime Minister, but what? We're out of infectious diseases and it's too cold for your plague of locusts idea.'

'Well, you know how they love celebrities? Can we get Joanna Lumley to protest about something? No, I have it! Get Peter Andre and Jordan to split up! They can always get together again in a couple of weeks on the cover of *Hello!* magazine, and we get a bit of breathing space. Get me Max Clifford, now!'

24 May 2009

QUIET, PLEASE

If the French Open championships have taught the tennis fan anything this year, with the Queen's tournament and Wimbledon upon us, it's that it is time to stock up, not just on earplugs, but on earmuffs, balaclavas and possibly deerstalkers with the flaps down. Nothing to do with the chances of Sir Cliff breaking into song again – rather it's the screaming and the shrieking.

Anyone watching the tennis from Paris for the past two weeks might be excused for thinking that they'd tuned into an 'adult' channel by mistake. Maria Sharapova has been a serial offender for years, growing ever louder and more hysterical in her cries with every passing championship; but nowadays everybody's at it. A recent ladies' match at the French was like a deafening dawn chorus, with Dinara Safina squawking like a terrified waterhen, and on the other side of the net Victoria Azarenka emphasising every shot like a goose with the croup. Even the men are adding bird impressions to every passing shot: last week's Andy Murray versus Fernando González game sounded like a struggle between two startled pheasants. It's a far cry, in more ways than one, from the Corinthian days of Bunny Austin and Suzanne Lenglen. You never heard as much as a whimper from Ann Jones, and Björn Borg had all the verbal reaction of a cigar-store Indian. Even old John McEnroe didn't shout when he hit the ball, only when he missed.

Is it too late to plead for a return to more gracious ways? The Centre Court has rejected the Mexican wave and spurned the French handclap; can we hope that the only extraneous sound to be heard on court this year will be the applause when the umpire asks the crowd to turn off their mobile phones?

High-pitched screams apart, Maria Sharapova's assets are well known enough without further embellishment here, but in the final set of a game early last week she called on the trainer, who proceeded to massage her upper thigh for several minutes. A listener remarked, as the camera dwelt lovingly on this scene, that there was a job that he wouldn't mind doing. It reminded him of the Woody Allen line in the film *What's New Pussycat?*: 'I've got a job dressing the girls at the local strip club – 20 francs a week – it's not much . . . but it's all I can afford.'

7 June 2009

STONE ME

This week, it's been heartening to see the media achieve a decent balance between light and shade. The more serious news stories, such as Royal Ascot hats and frocks and Andy Murray's new shorts, have been leavened by news of carrots, sticklebacks and woolly mammoths. The *Today* programme on Radio 4 devoted much of their hard-edged news show to a learned discussion on the superior health-giving qualities of the boiled, as against the raw, sliced carrot. Madonna and Gwyneth Paltrow, much of whose lives appear to be given over to raw vegetables, must be distraught . . . Then, 'research showed' that your common or garden stickleback leaves the haughty salmon and turbot in the shade when it comes down to everyday piscine intelligence. Although, as a listener pointed out, not quite intelligent enough to avoid being caught. As for the woolly mammoth, the researchers have dug deep into the primeval and found that Dumbo's ancestor only trumpeted its last as little as 15,000 years ago. Perhaps they could be with us yet, if they'd known to boil their carrots.

However, the news story that became the cynosure of all eyes was President Obama sending a fly to its eternal reward during a television interview. 'Stone me!', as Tony Hancock used to say . . . As ever, there were those who sit by their television waiting to be offended. One such wrote to me, wondering how Mr Obama could on the one hand release the Guantanamo detainees, and at the same time indulge in blatant insecticide.

The unsavoury incident reminded another listener of an occasion when the great Scots comedian Chic Murray was in a waiting room, idly perusing a 10-year-old magazine, when he noticed a bluebottle buzzing around. He watched it for a few moments, and when it settled near him, dispatched it with a severe blow of the magazine. All activity in the room stopped suddenly, as shocked eyes turned on Chic. 'What?' he said. 'What? Was it a pet or something?'

'And finally', as Sir Trevor used to put it so well, there was the BBC weather girl, dispensing with the trivia, and explaining the Royal Ascot dress code to the great unwashed, finishing with 'trainers are not allowed anywhere'. Seemed a little harsh on a group whose services to racing were hitherto thought to be indispensable. Does Stoker Devonshire know about this?

21 June 2009

IT AIN'T HALF HOT, MAMAN

'Where are the snows of yesteryear?' cried Proust, or someone not unlike him. And how all those unfortunates who suffered heatstroke at Wimbledon last week would have agreed with him. 'It's too 'ot for me!' is the cry from a million British throats whenever we're lucky enough to get more than a couple of sunny days. Truly, we get the weather we deserve. Although what I did to deserve being born, live and marry in the rains of Ireland, I'd like to know.

At the moment, however, you find me sitting in the shade somewhere in south-west France, not far from where D'Artagnan was born; but since he was a fictional character, that may well be a French joke to fox the foreigner, particularly if he's *anglais*. It's a moot point whether the French scorn us more than they do the Americans, but they certainly find our sense of humour a puzzlement. There's a lovely little town nearby named Condom, where passing British tourists pose against the road sign, pointing and laughing heartily. The French look on, bemused: 'Zut! The mad Brits! It's their bad weather and terrible food. Gets to their brains you know.'

Well, *mes amis*, we're not alone in our eccentricity. The other evening I strayed into a little bistro in a traditionally deserted French village which, as ever, posed the question, 'Where is everybody?'

Anyway, this little restaurant in the middle of nowhere gave forth a blast of Brazilian music as we entered, then a smiling boy from Ipanema led us to our table and pressed a caipirinha cocktail upon us, while a merry matron roguishly took our order, singing and shimmying to the insistent rhythms of the Copacabana. And so it went, South American merrymaking on all sides, at least for the first hour and a half, by which time we'd just got our starter.

Then the music changed, from merry Jobim to moody Brel, and with it went the service and the staff. Cariocas who had been banging the tambourine while dishing up the vittles were moodily smoking and mixing their own cocktails, and the fat lady had sung her last. We left, nearly four hours after we'd come in. I've always wanted to see Rio; I don't think I'll bother now. They do this kind of thing much better in Ireland.

5 July 2009

TIGHTENING OUR BELTS

As the next wave of television ballroom dancing threatens to engulf the viewer (why does every half-decent television idea have to die the death of a thousand cuts?), it's heartening to see that cookery shows still have some life left in them. *Simple Suppers, Britain's Best Dish, Come Dine With Me, The Hairy Bikers' Food Tour of Britain* and many more are there to whet our appetites. It can only be a matter of time before Gordon, Marco Pierre and Raymond start hurling the skillets around again on prime time to bring out the gourmet in all of us.

But just in case we all get too carried away with rolling our own pasta, it was good to be brought back down to earth with the news that Whitehall is drawing up plans to issue every household kitchen with a slop bucket. The better part of our leftovers will be collected by binmen and sent to recycling plants. Whether this means we're on the threshold of a thrifty food revolution – where we'll be able to buy the recycled baked beans we threw out last week, or the reconstituted remains of last Monday's cottage pie – remains to be seen. In these belt-tightening times, good husbandry of our resources is the message, and is suitably reflected in yet another television cookery show, *Economy Gastronomy*.

The aim is to show ordinary families how to drastically cut back on their weekly food budget by cooking the aforementioned slops and turning them into delicious and nutritious meals. The two thrifty cookery gurus in charge promise that you can throw a slap-up lunch party for family and friends for about £2.50 a head. How? By simply putting together all the leftovers you have in the larder and fridge! Simple.

Except that when you and I throw open the fridge or larder door, we find a tired lettuce, a slice of ham, a bit of cheese and a sad-looking tomato. The gurus' shelves, however, groan under the weight of every kind of food imaginable. Hurrah! Let's have the neighbours in as well! Just don't forget to add that pinch of salt.

If your larder is not bursting at the seams, you need look no further than the hedgerows, according to Hugh Fearnley-Whippingboy and his ilk. That's all very well, but take the humble blackberry. One grumpy friend wants to know why it is that when you're out walking the dog, there are hundreds of blackberries on the bushes one day; come the next and they've all rotted or disappeared? And why do all the good ones always lurk at the back, so that you end up all black, blue and bloody in search of these treasures?

20 September 2009

A MAD WORLD, MY MASTERS

A listener sends me a verbatim conversation from a recent visit to a greasy spoon near the Humber Bridge:

Customer: 'The Full English, please, but instead of the fried bread, could I just have a slice of ordinary bread?'

Waitress: 'No. Can't change the menu.'

Customer: 'But it's the same thing, just not fried.'

Waitress: 'Can't change the menu.'

Customer: 'Can't you just forget to fry it?'

Supervisor arrives.

Her: 'Can't change the menu. We can leave it off.'

Customer: 'But isn't that changing the menu?'

Her: 'Do you want it or not?'

Customer: 'Oh, OK. Pop it on . . .'

Didn't I read somewhere that the rest of the world, particularly France, is only in the ha'penny place, when compared to British food? Or was it service?

A countryman tells me that he lives in a part of the world where the council works for the people, not the other way around. I think it's called Utopia. So it always comes as a shock to this bumpkin, whenever he comes to London, to find that the reverse is true . . . Mr Hayseed parked his car at Leytonstone Tube station and got a 30 quid fine because he put his ticket on the dashboard instead of sticking it on a window. He subsequently lost the ticket but, since he had paid, appealed the fine. Waltham Forest council sent him a sharp letter, saying that he had failed to provide proof of payment. Enclosed was a photograph of his car. It included a close-up of the ticket, on the dashboard . . . My friend says that it's not unusual that in Britain today you can get a salary and a pension for this kind of thing.

*

And I've been told this story so often, I'm beginning to wonder if it mightn't be true. In pain, my friend rings the surgery, but can't get through (surprise!) and drives, in discomfort, to the doctor's. It's half-eight in the morning, but he can't make an appointment. The receptionist can't speak to him until half-nine, because phone calls take priority until then. 'I'll wait,' says my pain-wracked pal. Then a woman in the back of the queue says, 'But all the appointments might be gone by then!' A bulb flashes on over the sufferer's head. 'Supposing I ring you on my mobile phone?' Reluctantly, the receptionist agrees. He rings the surgery number. The receptionist ignores the phone. He moves his mobile from his ear and says, 'Excuse me, your phone is ringing'. The receptionist picks it up. 'Hello,' says my pal. 'Can I make an appointment?' He could, and did. At the end of the call, he says 'Bye, bye' on the phone. Looking him straight in the face, the receptionist replies, 'Bye, bye' . . . Funny old world.

4 October 2009

THINK BIKE!

'Think Bike!' the matrix sign over the motorway warned, just as another rocketing motorcyclist hurtled by at 100 miles an hour, inches from my car's wing mirror. Like the proverbial bat out of hell, he swerved from one lane to another, dicing with death in between cars, vans and lorries until his rear lights were out of sight. His only protective clothing was a helmet, otherwise a jacket, jeans and trainers. If he'd come off that bike at even 20 miles an hour he'd have had broken feet, legs, arms and carried the scars for the rest of his life, always providing he lived. Think Bike? Bike Think, more like . . .

Now, just in case you think I'm anti-bike, you're looking at a person who spent most of his formative years on a velocipede, accounting for my still formidable thews. Indeed, I spent so much time awheel, I was half-boy, half-bike, my atoms and the machine's having blended into one another, like Flann O'Brien's Third Policeman. The little roads of Ireland were mercifully free of other traffic then, and were mine to wheel about at will. This happy state of two-wheeled affairs has long since been overtaken by heavy traffic, but not, apparently, in the minds of today's cyclists. God's gift to our embattled environment, they obviously feel that they're doing enough to save us all from ourselves, and are therefore above such lowly considerations as observing the rules of the road. Traffic lights, one-way streets, stop signs, even pavements are only for lower-carbon-emitting mortals, such as motorists and pedestrians . . . Cyclists Rule.

On related matters, I'll be amazed if the latest doom-mongering about Arctic ice melting hasn't already been hotly disputed by other scientists, but it's a measure of how we've become inured to the constant cries of 'Wolf!' that the only reaction I've had from the Plain People of Britain has been to speculate that with the rising temperatures and the melting ice, we'll not drown. We'll just be gently poached.

Without so much as a by-your-leave, the Government hiked up car tax on high-emission cars, with no regard for thousands who drive such vehicles because of their livelihood, or where they live. They then made it retrospective for existing cars, as well as new ones. Now that Sir Thomas Legg has made MPs' new expenses rules retrospective, isn't it refreshing to see how our legislators have taken it on the chin, with the kind of unquestioning acceptance they expect from us?

18 October 2009

A ROYAL REQUEST

Far be it for me to decry the pomp and circumstance attending Her Majesty's delivery of The Queen's Speech, which is certainly the Monarch speaking, but otherwise is as much her own work as the commercial 'voice-overs' for television that I occasionally do to keep the wolf from the door. It is just that I, and every other motorist who had to endure the impenetrable logjam that was London's traffic last Wednesday, respectfully wish that you could find some way of sneaking into the Houses of Parliament without causing hours of traffic mayhem, Ma'am . . . Perhaps the river route, from Hampton Court, as favoured by Henry VIII?

I fully realise that the good Prince Philip and yourself – your passage from the Palace cleared by diligent police whose particular joy it is to stop the traffic – would have no idea of the chaos in your wake, but what about recording the thing from a comfortable room at the Palace, as you do your Christmas Message? If I told you that Millbank, on the main Embankment route, was closed, not only all of Wednesday but most of Thursday, would that in any way sway your decision for next year? Through no fault of yours, it's not as if the speech went well anyway, with the greatest respect, Ma'am. I'd let the Prime Minister take the rap in future. You'd earn the undying gratitude of every trucker, motorist, bus and taxi driver in London.

We're lucky with our taxi drivers, who know where they're going, however slowly. I once asked one in Los Angeles to take me to Beverly Hills, and he had to get out of the car to go to a phone box to get directions from the office. In Dublin, at a Eurovision Song Contest, I asked the taxi driver to take me to the broadcast centre. 'Oh!', he moaned, you would! That place full of police, and me without any road tax!' In Dublin again, I hear a driver take instruction from his controller: 'Up to the end of the road, Mick, and turn right at the "No Right Turn" sign.'

Not unlike Her Majesty, I too, have been accompanied through the streets of Dublin's fair city by a motorcycle escort, for another Eurovision contest. When we arrived at our destination, my driver slipped the sergeant in charge some crisp notes, and the escort immediately roared off to collect the Irish President . . .

And do you know, Ma'am, I don't remember giving a tinker's curse for the poor eejits held up at every set of traffic lights . . .

22 November 2009

HEY YEAH!

As they say in the best *Telegraph* letters pages, 'Am I alone . . .' in deeply resenting being addressed as 'mate', 'luv', 'darlin'' or, worst of all, 'guys', by those for whose services I'm paying through the nose? I mentioned this irritant in passing recently and by your response, it seems as if I may be leaning against an open door with many of you. 'So, what's it to be, guys?' is not what you want to hear while perusing the menu of a joint that's going to knock you back 60 quid a head.

The Irish, in a mistaken attempt at their far-famed hospitality, are particular offenders. I suppose it's because I'm one of them and I know they're only doing it because they want to make me welcome. I shouldn't get a tad eggy when I'm greeted by the receptionist of a hotel that is costing me €200 a night (with breakfast extra) with a cheery 'Howya?', but it does put me a little on edge. Nor do I appreciate the barman, whose vodka and tonic is going to cost me the best part of a tenner, greeting me with 'How's it goin'?', usually adding insult to injury with, 'would you like ice and lemon with that?' No, just pour it on the bar, and I'll lap it off . . .

I should be used to it. Many years ago in a Dublin restaurant a friend and I were civilly discussing the wine list, weighing a fruity Burgundy against a robust Bordeaux, when the waiter, tiring of the delay, interrupted, 'And what'll it be for booze?' Friends on a recent visit to Oban were sitting quietly in the Fish Restaurant of the Year for about two minutes when the waitress came over and said 'Are youz two ready tae order, or wha?' In Glasgow at lunchtime: 'What are you guys having today? French toast with fresh fruit? Yeah! Cool!'

It gets worse: witness a registrar of marriages, who tells me that he was somewhat taken aback at the very first marriage he conducted, when the groom greeted him with a breezy 'Wotcha, mate!' Then a magistrate capped them all, by telling of a prisoner who, as he left the dock, turned to the magistrates with a smile and a 'Thanks, guys!'

6 December 2009

MY FINAL FOND FAREWELL

Let me begin by quoting from a slim, little-read volume called *The Day Job*, written by my own fair hand in 1980. 'The most important date for me was in April 1972, when I took over the morning show on BBC Radio 2. Lots of people in the business and a number of critics were very sniffy and said that I wouldn't make it, that I was "wrong" for the morning, and the public wouldn't accept me. They were quite right, of course, but like the constant drip that I am, I have worn down their resistance. I'm still hanging on grimly, limpet-like, in the now-forlorn hope of acclaim and approbation . . .'

How prophetic. As I said to my friends – as I prefer to call my listeners – when I presented the Radio 2 breakfast show for the last time on Friday, I'm not going to miss the early mornings, when crocodiles still roam the streets. Nor will I pine for the dark and dreary winter months when I've finished my day's work and outside the BBC's hallowed, cigarette-strewn portals it's still as black as your grandfather's proverbial.

What I am going to miss is the fun and laughter. Every single morning, come rain or shine, whether I'd had a sleepless night, a streaming cold, or a horrendous hangover, I always had a smile on my face in my studio. I could always rely on my friends to see the funny side of things, whether we were in the grip of a three-day week, a miners' strike, the Falklands War, or the dreadful IRA bombing campaign that made life so difficult for every Irishman in Britain.

I could fill a book – and indeed have – with the extraordinary flights of fancy that my listeners and I have conjured up together in the 27 years I hosted the breakfast show.

I chuckled at Willy Gofar's attempt to balloon around the world in 80 days while keeping one foot securely on the ground. It was a project doomed from the start because of Willy's insistence on going home for his tea every evening.

People still remind me of the homely fun we shared in the eighties at the expense of *Dallas*, with its multi-billionaire oil barons who had walk-in cupboards and wire coat-hangers, only one telephone in the hall, and whose heads and bodies seemed to change with alarming frequency, apparently unnoticed by anybody else.

How the memories come flooding back of the Oil Barons' Ball, with the richest people in Texas huddled together in a small anteroom, the wind-blown swimming pool, and the lavish breakfasts at which JR would down a thimbleful of orange juice before ruining everybody's day. Bobby's dream in the shower finally put the tin stetson on all that.

In the nineties, do you remember the ongoing saga of the cones? Miles and miles of the little blighters with nary a soul working on the other side of them. My spies would report on cone farms with breeding pairs, one on top of the other. Nothing's changed, of course: there are more cones on our roads than ever. The infamous Cones Hotline, which invited us to 'phone in with our complaints', failed to trouble the starter. The Highways Agency wound it up. Apparently, all our complaints were wrong, so there.

Between 1972 and 1984, my listeners banded together under the banner of the Terry Wogan is Tops Society, or Twits. Then I left, in a marked manner, for a three-nights-a-week stint on TV with my chat show, *Wogan*. I did eight and a bit years of that, and the only thing people remember about it is George Best being drunk.

I thought that it had run its course after about seven years, but the powers that be at the time assured me that it was invaluable, so I stayed on. Meanwhile, they were building an entire village in Spain called Eldorado with which to replace me . . .

You learn as you go along. So I returned to radio and my listeners rallied, this time as Terry's Old Geezers, or Togs. Over the years they have formed into a formidable force for good, raising millions for Children in Need, with calendars, cake stalls, quizzes, conventions and particularly the selling of the infamous Janet and John CDs, recordings of simple tales of honest folk that reduce listeners to helpless laughter for reasons that escape me.

A previous incumbent of the poisoned chalice that is the controllership of Radio 2 was once heard to describe *Wake Up to Wogan* as just 'food and filth'. Well, she was right about the food. Shameless pleading over the years has led to a steady flow of vittles and provender that have helped keep my blood sugar levels steady.

In fact, I'm thinking of opening a corner store. One day while on air last week saw the arrival of an enormous Melton Mowbray pie, sausage rolls, mince pies, cupcakes and four large bags containing naan bread, poppadoms, saffron rice, chicken tikka and the rest of an Indian feast. We ate it all – it would have been rude not to – and a snap of the fingers to the begrudgers who cry: 'How can you eat curry at eight o'clock in the morning?' Watch me. I'm lucky, of course. I can eat anything I like without putting on a pound. Probably nerves . . .

As I've said before, we have a propensity to confuse longevity with merit. In my business, if you can stay sober and upright for long enough, a small proportion of the public will look upon you with what almost amounts to affection. And that's the point at which you should count your blessings and silently steal away. So, dear listener, until we meet again in February for a new mid-morning show on Sundays, full to bursting with live music, fun and, with any luck, more food, let me reverse the old Roman hurrah, Vale . . . *atque ave*! Farewell . . . and hail!

20 December 2009

FA LA LA LA LA!

So, kiddies, here we are at The Winter of Our Discontent or, as it's better known, Christmas. The lights have been lit on London's Oxford and Regent Streets this many a week and, as anybody who has taken a car, bus or taxi down either thoroughfare for the past month will know, you've had plenty of time to look at the lights.

Still, curmudgeonly references to the Season of Goodwill have been out of date since Dickens invented Scrooge, so apart from wondering why anybody bothers with Christmas pudding – a stodgy cannon ball that sits on top of your undigested turkey, ham and all the trimmings like a lump of concrete – let us be jolly, fa la la la la. The parson's nose goes to all begrudgers who moan about how the 'Real Spirit of Christmas' has been ruined by over-commercialisation. Just because there's always the mother and father of a row at the Mitchell 'Faaamly' party at the Queen Vic doesn't mean that every family's Christmas dinner is an excuse for a punch-up. Despite what some sour-pussed tabloid feature writers may want you to believe, not every family in the country throws a dysfunctional fit at this time of the year.

Mind you, I get a bit testy when, as Father of the Feast, nobody takes a blind bit of notice of my demands that there be an end to excessive conspicuous consumption. 'One Man, One Present!' Ha! The present Lady Wogan behaves like a sailor on shore leave, and the rest of my family take their lead from her, ignoring that austere old penny-pincher in the corner. 'Give him another drink and a drumstick. He'll be asleep in a minute . . .' God bless the days when, banjaxed with food, I'd lie on the floor of the dining room, waiting to explode. Older and wiser, it is now but the work of a moment for a kindly grandchild to help me to an easy chair.

Ah, memories. Trying to assemble a Wendy house for my daughter on Christmas Eve, while the worse for drink. My Aunty Nelly dishing up the turkey in the granny's kitchen in Dublin with her traditional cry: 'Now, take your time, youse are not rushin' for a bus.' My great and sorely missed friend Tom, with the hard stuff lapping up against his teeth, attempting to throw the butt of his Christmas Eve cigar out the door of his car and following it into the street. The car, sliding back down the hill, pursued by my inebriated friend, is something that will remain to warm my cockles, and indeed my Brussels, for now and all my Christmases to come. And may all your days be merry and bright . . .

27 December 2009

THE FOLDED TENT

Ever since I bade a fond 'hors d'oeuvre' to my loyal band of listeners, the present Lady Wogan has been receiving solicitous calls from her kindly friends: 'And how is Terry? Is he all right?' The wrong person to ask of course, since nobody knows my failings better than herself. It's just that, ingrate that I am, I feel like shouting, 'Give the boy a chance! I've retired from getting up while the cocks are still snoring their beaks off of a morning, that's all. I'm abed a little longer, OK?' (Although, with the weather, and the total incompetence of local and district councils, I certainly picked the right time to quit trudging through the snow). There's nothing wrong with me, I haven't seen hide nor hair of the Grim Reaper, and I was feeling perfectly well, until you asked. Now, I'm feeling a twinge . . .

'Retirement' has got a bad name, and not just because of the numpties who've made a mess of our pensions. We fear the lack of reason to get out of bed, the day stretching pointlessly before us. Do we really want to play golf every day? Or bowls, or bridge, or darts? Is it to be tea, toast and Titchmarsh every afternoon? The great hunter-gatherer dozes fitfully by the fire. Oh, for the boredom of the office, the merry camaraderie as we stand together on freezing platforms waiting for the train that never comes. Leaves on the line, wrong sort of rain, too fluffy snow . . . gone, gone for ever.

As ever, or so the sisters are at pains to tell us, it's the women who bear the real burden. Your man under her feet all day, and loath to lift his own for the vacuum cleaner. Following the good woman around the supermarket, questioning her every purchase, getting into a strop trying to open those infuriating little plastic bags. In the kitchen every lunchtime, getting in the way. Demanding to know what the hell has happened to the screwdriver/

hammer/torch. Ruining a True Movies weepie in the afternoon with sarky comments . . .

Be of good cheer, my retiring friends. There is a light at the end of the tunnel – and you know it won't be a train, in this weather. One of my dearest friends positively glories in his retirement, so relieved that he no longer might kill somebody. He's a doctor. Come on, me hearties! It's a load off your shoulders, take the weight off your feet. As John Wayne said, 'Sit a spell, and let your saddle cool . . .'

And stay out of the kitchen. And the supermarket.

3 January 2010

WAG TALES

What a week to be a WAG! And what a week to be Alison Kervin, a sports writer who has just published a book on that very subject, identical excerpts from which could be avidly read in most newspapers. Timing, it's a gift.

And what do we learn of these pampered lovelies, living lives of luxury in their mansions and impeccable gardens, set well behind the gates and walls that would keep out the most zealous paparazzo? Are they enjoying a lotus-eating life of unrestrained pleasure, pink champagne in the jacuzzi to start the day, the spa in the afternoon, and every night on the town in the trendiest clubs with the 'lads' and fellow WAGS? Ha! That's what you think.

They're lonely, bored and afraid. And it's not because they're not being asked to lunch or bridge by snooty neighbours in Oxshott or Alderley Edge, because most of them are footballers' wives as well. They're desperately unhappy playing second-best to football clubs that only care about their husbands, and they're pale with the exhaustion of worrying about what their husbands are getting up to when the big gates close behind them.

According to Ms Kervin, they're right to worry. She paints a frightening picture of half-naked young women flinging themselves on defenceless, vulnerable footballers at every turn. Even when the wives are present, they have to fight tooth and nail to defend their poor spouses from the wiles of these harpies. It's hell, but does nobody spare a thought for the footballer? To whom does he turn in these stressful moments? Well, of course, Max Clifford; but what if the wife/girlfriend has got there first?

This sad, no, pathetic state of affairs has been brought into sharp relief by the 'Terry' revelations. Frankly, when I saw the headlines first, I thought that they'd finally got something on me, and was booking the one-way to Rio, before herself read the rest of the article to me.

As I write this, the papers are taking a high moral tone and shifting all responsibility onto the England coach, Fabio Capello. 'Sack Terry as England captain?' If I were Capello, I would have made an excuse about a sick aunt and hidden out in Naples. It's football, stupid . . . In the Shed at Stamford Bridge they'll be singing hymns and arias to their hero's virility, and who do you think will get the biggest cheer when England next play at Wembley? Think again, Capello. If it happened in Italy, Terry could run for President.

7 February 2010

ME-TIME

With that mid-season boon to the greetings card industry, Valentine's Day, on us even as we speak, it's only right and proper that we should have been inundated on an hourly basis by surveys on 'What Women Want' from their loved ones on the big day. A handwritten romantic poem or letter would appear to be the ideal. Failing that, a passing compliment on the lady's appearance (and remember, on this day of all days the answer to the question, 'Does my bum look big in this?' is always a resounding 'No!') or, and this may seem a little desperate, 'some lingering eye contact'. Pursuing this quaint idea of the easily pleased woman, a good third of the females questioned said that they would be 'disappointed' if asked to pay for their share of their Valentine's dinner. For heaven's sake woman, dump the cheapskate! No romance is worth going dutch on a Big Mac.

However, a 'relationship expert' says that while men may no longer be knights in shining armour, and damsels in distress are in similarly short supply, we still crave romance. The 'expert' goes on to say: 'The beauty of romance in the twenty-first century is that it's a blank slate. Forget about everyone else, and make Valentine's Day work for YOU.'

I thought so. It's the answer to everything these days, even a maiden's prayer: Me, Me, Me. And here we pause for the familiar mantra: 'If you don't love yourself, how can you love anybody else?'

Get back to the ashram, guru. Self-love or self-regard is not the same as self-esteem; it's the opposite. Self-regard is the open door to vanity, pride, narcissism and arrogance, so much in evidence, and indeed admired, nowadays as necessary qualities on the onward march towards 'celebrity', stardom and riches. When I was growing up, and it wasn't during the War of the Spanish

Succession, the 'show-off' was a pariah, the boastful shunned. Nobody punched the air or ripped off their shirt when they scored a goal or a try. Believe it or not, modesty was thought of as a virtue. It might be hard to prove, but I'm willing to bet that Hitler had plenty of self-regard, but little self-esteem. Indeed, I'd be surprised if we couldn't say the same about many politicians. Or footballers. Or radio and television . . . but no, I've gone far enough. That Chinese emperor had the right idea, being followed everywhere by a eunuch whose job it was, every time the Big Man got above himself, to whisper in the emperor's ear: 'Remember, you too are human.' Might be worth a try, Simon.

14 February 2010

IF IT AIN'T BROKE . . .

For years, the holy grail for radio and television producers and controllers has been 'Yoof'. The Jesuits' supposed catchphrase 'Give me a child before the age of seven and I'll have them for life' is obviously the philosophy behind the broadcast media's relentless search for the Elusive Youth of 18–25-year-olds. And for what seems like a similar number of years, wise old heads have been pointing out the sad but true fact that the Elusive Youth is but a pipe dream, a mirage that simply isn't there. At least, not as far as radio and television are concerned.

'Yoof' is somewhere else, listening to an iPod, or otherwise Googling, Yahooing, Tweeting. And at peak-viewing times on the weekend clubbing or pubbing. What they're not doing is sitting with the family watching telly. How to grab them and nail them to the chair has exercised the finest brains in the media, and many are the broken executives who have retired to the safer havens of gardening and *A House in the Country*.

Extraordinary, then, that the only radio and television network to have actually succeeded in attracting a younger audience is being instructed to kick the golden ball into touch and search diligently for the older listener! You and I, dear listener, will remember the days when BBC Radio 2 was regarded as Radio 1's poor, raddled relation. Middle of the Road, middle-aged, middling. Over the last 15 years, by dint of hard work, enlightened controllers, a popular music policy, the employment of producers and presenters whose hearts and minds were dedicated to radio, poor old Radio 2 became the popular broadcasting giant it is today. The corporation's most successful network, which the most recent listening figures show has by far the biggest listening audience in Britain, Europe and possibly the known universe, is being instructed to change its ways. Too popular, you see, spoiling things for commercial radio. More culture, that's the ticket. More old folk. It's that familiar maxim again: if it ain't broke, break it . . .

Radio 4's coming in for a bit of a kicking as well, being accused of 'dumbing-down' *Desert Island Discs*. For heaven's sake, I've been a castaway twice, first with that grand man who thought it all up, Roy Plomley. The secret of its success is that every listener would love to be on the Island, and to impress the nation with the breadth of their musical taste. Many have yellowing lists in their pockets, just in case they're invited. Somewhere up there, dear Roy is guffawing heartily. He invented a simple, brilliant programme format. It's popular light entertainment, not 'culture'.

Thank goodness.

21 February 2010

A STOIC AT LARGE

As you know, you'll never hear a whimper from me, although, since a rugby injury 50 years ago, I am rarely without pain. When it comes to stoicism, Marcus Aurelius was only in the ha'penny place, compared with yours truly. Mother's Brave Little Soldier I was known in my time, for my dogged refusal to scream, except in extremis, such as a Chinese burn, cramp, or, in later years, the tearing of a plaster from a hairy leg.

Four weeks ago they took away my left knee and replaced it with plastic, set in a bed of ready-mix concrete. Since then I have learnt that what I previously thought was pain was a bagatelle, a passing zephyr. At regular intervals the reincarnation of Torquemada, posing as a charming physiotherapist, puts me through the worst excesses of the Spanish Inquisition, including her interpretation of the bastinado. Next time we meet you'll find me a good three inches taller, particularly on the left-hand side.

As soon as you dispense with the crutches, people's sympathy drifts away as the idle wind. Last Tuesday, as I limped gamely to the podium at the Grosvenor House hotel to receive an award as The Prettiest Face on Radio, or some such, I heard what can only be described as sharp intakes of breath.

Or, it could have been sniggering; I've been getting a lot of awards lately, in the hope that I'll take the hint and not come back, and it must be getting on people's nerves. As I sat at my table, various ladies approached me for a photo. I apologised at being unable to stand, due to my bad knee, and, to a woman, they offered to sit on it. Why do these things never happen when you're a young fella, and in the full of your health?

14 March 2010

IRELAND'S COOLEST MAN

On the well-established principle that 'you can't please all of the people all of the time', only the veriest dub or consummate 'eejit' would imagine himself universally acclaimed. Indeed, in my case I detect a groundswell of opinion, as I remarked upon last week, that one more award to yours truly, and they'll be rushing the platform. So it was with mixed feelings that I awoke on a sunny St Patrick's Day morning to find myself acclaimed 'Ireland's Coolest Man'. And this in the face of the sternest opposition: Pierce Brosnan, Colin Farrell and Christine Bleakley, although what she was doing in there remains a mystery. Before anybody loses the run of themselves, this was a poll conducted in this country, for British voters. A similar poll conducted in Ireland would produce a much different result, and I doubt that myself, Pierce, Colin or even Christine would get a look-in.

The Irish are not that big on 'celebrity' or status, or those placed in authority over them. 'Howya, Bertie?' was the usual greeting for the former Prime Minister, the Hon. Mr Ahern, and the present Taoiseach, the Hon. Mr Cowan, is known to all and sundry by his nickname, 'Biffo' (Big Ignorant Fellow from Offaly), except of course that 'fellow' is not the word commonly used.

Enough respect? Never, in Ireland. I'm reminded of a former President of Ireland, Sean T. O'Kelly, an honest and good man, but short, very short, of stature. In the tradition of all Irish presidents, even to the present day, when the duty is performed by the outstanding current president, Mary McAleese, Sean T. O'Kelly greeted both teams of a rugby or football international on the pitch. He always cut an elegant figure, in Crombie overcoat and homburg hat. And as he walked along, shaking each player warmly by the hand, as one voice the crowd would shout, 'Cut the grass! Where is he?!' Poor man, he wasn't that small.

When I was growing up, the Irish didn't even make much of a fuss of St Patrick. You wore a sprig of shamrock and a little tinsel harp, you went to Mass, and while children had a day off school, grown-ups could forget the Lenten fast and get some proper drink and food inside themselves. The only parades were in Boston, New York or Chicago, where they dyed the rivers green, and the police and Ancient Order of Hibernians marched behind pipe bands. We couldn't even imagine it. Now that Ireland has outgrown the isolated penury of the hungry years, all its cities and towns celebrate the good saint's name in famous fashion. Music, dancing, laughter, the 'craic'. Any chance of a quiet pint, without some gobdaw singing in your ear? That'd be 'cool'.

21 March 2010

IF YOU WANT TO GET AHEAD . . .

You may have missed it, but last Tuesday was 'World Turban Day', an invitation from the Sikh Turban Pride Organisation to all their male co-religionists to stop cutting their hair and trimming their beards and get back to basics by rewinding the old turban around the head as usual.

'A big turban may make it difficult to play cricket, but a Sikh without a turban is like a king without a crown,' said the religion's supreme spiritual leader. Which puts a lot of pressure on Monty Panesar. Putting aside the point that Her Majesty does not feel the need to wear her crown every day, and that we've never seen the crowned heads of Europe wearing theirs, Sikh men have been wearing turbans ever since 1699, when a great guru of the time prohibited them from cutting their hair, gave everyone the surname Singh (Lion) and insisted that they each wear a steel bangle, long cotton underwear, a wooden comb and a sheathed sword. I can't speak for the bangle or the comb, and I wouldn't care to speculate about the underwear, but very few Sikhs of my acquaintance are going about with an uncomfortable sheathed sword in their back pocket.

Incidentally, as a Freeman of the City of London, I'm entitled to stroll about the place with my sword unsheathed. I use it sparingly, to discourage hawkers, muggers and politicians . . . Well, I'm all for the turban. I'm all for the Sikhs, who seem to find an excuse for a party or a festival every couple of weeks.

And while they're bringing back the turban, any chance that we could reintroduce the hat? Look at the photos of great political gatherings from the early part of the twentieth century: every man-jack of the milling throng is sporting a titfer. From my childhood to sometime in the sixties, no self-respecting male put his nose outside the door without his hat. 'If you want to get ahead, get a hat,' was the watchword. You never saw a cowboy without one. You took off your hat as you entered, put it back on as you left. Everybody knew whether you were coming or going, including yourself.

Just look at that wildly acclaimed US TV series *Mad Men*. What is it that gives the man that all others envy, Don Draper, his magnetic force? It's the hat. He never leaves home, mistress or martini without it. When he takes off his hat, people listen. When he puts it on, they stand up. It seems to carry an almost religious force. Which is where we came in . . .

18 April 2010

SHOWING THEIR COLOURS

Yellow. It's the new black. And we owe it all to the Lib Dems or, more specifically, Clegg's tie. Frankly, it's a shade too tarty for me, but it has set the fashion world alight, at least until they come up with something new next week. And you thought it was confined to canaries, Delia Smith and Norwich City? Kate Moss has been seen in yellow, and Her Majesty the Queen. Although I doubt if we'll see SamCam flaunting it, or Gordon's missus. If they do, we'll know power-sharing is really on the cards. Still, it's a peculiar choice of colour for a political party; yes, it's the colour of the sun, but it's also the colour of the flag flown when there was plague aboard ship, me hearties. And in countless Western movies it stood for shameful cowardice: 'Go for your gun! Or are you too yella, Kincaid?' On the other hand, the Japanese associate it with courage (the Yellow Peril) and, let's not forget, Homer Simpson's yellow.

You can see the problem for the Lib Dems: the Tories and Labour had nailed blue and red, way back when. Anybody remember what colour were the Whigs? But the Lib Dems couldn't pick black (Nazi colour) or white (Pope's got that one), so what's left? Of course, there are orange and green, but they've been a cause of trouble in Ireland for years.

Why not fawn, taupe, beige: colours favoured by the silent middle-aged majority? Votes there for the taking, I fancy. Or silver, for those with 'Silver threads among the gold . . .' Speaking of which, why didn't they go for gold? Or pink, shocking pink. Now that would be a fashion statement. Think about it for next time, Nick . . .

Gordon's already gone pink, bright pink, since his Rochdale debacle. Of course he's entitled to his opinion, just as that woman he called a 'bigot' is entitled to hers, but not if he wants her vote.

His defenders will say that the election is supposed to be about substance, not style, something we can all agree on, except for the sad fact that this one, with its televised debates and relentless 24-hour media coverage, is being fought, and will be won, in the glare of television lights and microphones that pick up every little careless aside. When you work in television you have to learn, quickly, that the 'mic' on your lapel or tie is not necessarily switched off by 'sound' immediately you're off-stage. I'm not the only one who has taken a live microphone with me into the loo.

Even if they're not attached, today's microphones will pick up the flutter of a butterfly's wings a mile away. It happened to Prince Charles over Nicholas Witchell. They both got over it, in time. So will the woman in Rochdale, but time is running out for Gordon.

2 May 2010

ELECTION NIGHT SPECIAL

I'll come clean. I didn't vote, so you can't blame me. And it wasn't because some jobsworth slammed a polling station door in my face, either. It was a baggage-handlers' 'go-slow' at Rome airport that stopped me exercising my franchise. Incidentally, how can you tell a baggage-handler's 'go-slow' from his usual pace? But I digress, and I'll bet you wish you could have found an excuse to leave the country, with or without your baggage, when you woke up and saw the damage on Friday morning. Was there ever before an election result that made no one in the country happy? Like yourself, and the rest of the plain people of Britain, I watched the television with mounting horror on Thursday night, until merciful sleep overtook me at about one o'clock on Friday morning. By then, absolutely nothing had happened, apart from in Sunderland where, obviously, the bean-counters have got two pairs of hands each. Although it's hard to believe that some constituencies still hadn't totted up their returns 12 hours later. Who were they using to count their votes, a short-sighted retired bank manager with a child's abacus? Mind you, there was plenty to see, if not enjoy, in those hiatus hours when, all over the country, Sunderland excepted, nothing was happening. Plenty of room for comment and opinion, and riveting reports about nothing from unfortunates standing out in the cold while they awaited Big Gordy and the wife in Kirkcaldy, and following the slow progress of Cameron's car to his local pub, into which the poor reporter was then refused entry. Much talk of how the 'exit poll' could well be all wrong, in view of what was seen as a 'swing' to the Tories. Well, the poll was right and the swing swung, but not high enough.

Of course, there were moments to lift the spirits, however briefly: Paxman in cheery mood, treating it all as if it were slightly beneath him; Dimbleby growing testier by the minute, answering Jeremy's call of 'Get on with it!' with a sharp 'Well, it will be a while before I come back to you!' Who could blame his mood, reduced as he was to asking Rory Cellan-Jones to read out 'tweets' from Twitter. Andrew Neil, wandering like a lost soul on a bobbing boat under the London Eye, asking 'celebrities' their dotty opinions, and coming up with a winner in Joan Collins, only for Tessa Jowell to ruin the moment with the dreaded slur, 'Botoxed!' when Andrew handed back to Paxman.

Still, it was one up on ITV, who only had Piers Morgan and Alastair Campbell sitting out in the cold, while Mary Nightingale let them get away with murder.

And finally, what does Lord Mandelson mean when he says that it's a vote for 'change'? Machiavelli himself wouldn't have chanced his arm with that one.

9 May 2010

THE ETERNAL CITY

Just getting my land legs back after a brief five days before the mast on the good ship *Queen Victoria*, where my loyal listeners once again came up trumps, raising money for Children in Need. I thought it best not to wear out my welcome by being on board for the duration of the 'TOGs Voyage', so I was piped aboard (or it could have been a raspberry) at Rome – well, to be absolutely accurate, Civitavecchia, which is as far from Rome as most Ryanair airports are from their destinations.

The Eternal City is ever magnificent, but exhausting. Too much to see in too short a time – a time that might be even shorter if you don't keep your eye on the traffic in the middle of the road, onto which you've been forced by the heaving crowd on the narrow pavements. The Piazza del Popolo lived up to its name, there wasn't an inch of space to be found on a Spanish Step. You could certainly throw a coin into the Trevi Fountain, if you felt you could hit the target over the heads of the crowd, from 200 metres away.

'*Bella figura*' is what the Italians like to think they cut, but this was the worst-dressed collection I've seen since I watched a Thomson flight disembark at Alicante airport. Rome is where a blighter on a scooter once tried to take the coat off my wife's back, foolishly not allowing for the lady's ability to punch above her weight. He survived, with minor contusions. Rome was where a woman asked me for an autograph while His Holiness was giving it large on Vatican Square. And if you've ever been there on such an occasion, you'll know to scoff at one of the great myths of our time: the assertion of certainty with the apparently unanswerable question, 'Has the Pope a balcony?' Well, the answer is 'No'. The Pope doesn't have a balcony; it's a window ledge. Where this leaves 'Bears doing their business in the woods', or the 'gun-shy Kennedys', I don't know. Just another little erosion into all that we hold dear.

Meanwhile, back on Blighty's shore, *'plus ça change'*, as they say in Limerick. Capital gains, Cheryl's divorce, an Irish Robin Hood, another movie featuring those four awful women from *Sex and the City*, endless television coverage of the Chelsea Flower Show and an opportunity to buy a limited edition of a book of photographs of Kate Moss for £327. Nurse! The screens . . .

30 May 2010

LA VIE EN ROSE

This week I've been in deepest France, with bullfrogs bellowing me to sleep at night and crickets disturbing the peace all day. As I stood in the swimming pool one of the little blighters floated by, struggling for its life to escape a watery grave. With the kind of respect for all God's creatures for which I've never been noted, unless they can be boiled, roasted or deep-fried, I helped the little grasshopper-type thing onto dry land. It must have been mightily relieved that some Giant Hand had saved its bacon at the last minute before the waters closed over its head. Motionless for a while, catching its breath, then slowly it began to shake a leg, then a wing, drying itself in the sun. After a couple of minutes, Jiminy Cricket was ready to face the world again. Powerful little legs extended, wings now dry and whirring, he suddenly took off, and with a graceful backflip, landed straight in the watery grave once more.

I've noticed that pheasants have the same foolish disregard for life and limb. You stop the car to allow the handsome bird to reach the safety of the hedgerow then, as soon as you start forward again, out it pops, straight under your wheels. And remember, you can't stop to check whether the poor thing might be suitable for the pot. It's the next man's roadkill. Play the game. It's not just insects or animals, we all know people like that. Indeed, but for the grace of another Giant Hand, there go most of us. Some people you just can't help – as soon as you pull them out of the water, they're straight back in. And some don't swim any better than crickets.

And in answer to the question I can hear bubbling on your lips, I did pick the cricket with a death wish out of the water once more, and set him on dry land yet again. Once again I watched as he shook himself dry a second time, obviously congratulating

124

himself on his good fortune at cheating the Grim Reaper not once, but twice. He probably thought of himself as indestructible, 'the cricket they couldn't kill', as this time, in one bound, he shot into the air in the opposite direction and off into the wide blue yonder. Probably straight into the jaws of a big bullfrog.

6 June 2010

MEMORIES AND MIRACLES

A hundred swans swim elegantly under Sarsfield Bridge as the great Shannon river flows towards the Atlantic. I'm in my native city in Ireland, Limerick.

Before you ask, nobody ever wrote a limerick in Limerick – unless it was about rugby. For this is the spiritual home of the Irish game, with its temple, Thomond Park, where mighty Munster play. The slogan across the grandstand reads, 'Irish by birth, Munster by the grace of God'. It's a good deal more than a mere game, here. Everybody plays; as the local saying goes, 'from docker to doctor'.

A soft rain beats steadily down – no surprise to someone like me, who was born here, in a shower. They say our childhood memories are only of the sunny days. Not if you were born in Limerick. I had more or less constant drizzle in my face and down the back of my neck as I cycled back and forth to school each day. When the film of Frank McCourt's book *Angela's Ashes*, which told of a family's poverty in the Limerick of the forties and fifties, came to the cinemas, I had people complaining to me about the exaggerated amount of rain lashing down throughout the film. I pointed out that the amount of stuff falling from the heavens was, if anything, understated.

I'm filming a documentary about Ireland, and my brother, Brian, came down from Dublin on the train so that we could reminisce together about the old times: the Da's grocery store, the little house where we spent our early days. As I met the brother at the railway station, a warm-hearted local shook me by the hand, and asked what I was up to. I told him, and he looked puzzled. 'Why couldn't they have got an Irishman to do it?' he asked. When a young man came up and asked me for 25 euros for his train fare, I knew that I was back home.

I came to my home town from Ballinspittle in County Cork where, you may vaguely remember, a statue of the Virgin Mary appeared to the devout to be moving about . . . This remarkable event became an international sensation, and very quickly thousands were flocking to the little shrine to kneel and pray, hoping to spot the concrete statue on the move. Many thousands will swear, to this day, that they saw the miracle. The less religious make the point that Ireland at the time, 1985, was in desperate economic trouble, and in need of inspiration – some sign that, if not the International Monetary Fund, at least the Mother of God was on their side.

In the present, even worse dire straits, they're looking closely at that statue again.

11 July 2010

IRISH ROSES

The fuchsia and honeysuckle sparkle in the rainy hedges of West Cork and South Kerry, as I continue to make my way around the coast of Ireland. Valentia Island, from where the first coaxial cable linked the Old World with the New in the nineteenth century, and communication between the two continents became instant, and eager stockbrokers in Britain and Europe got the news of the latest from the New York Exchange in minutes, rather than days. Which is where, you could say, our current financial problems began. Across the little bridge that separates the island from the mainland is Portmagee, a village with a name which sounds like it has emigrated from Northern Ireland, where the seafood leaps from the shore onto your plate, and the 'craic' in the bar is mighty. Song and dance, fiddle and bodhran, you'd never know there was a Depression. Except for the faces of the instrumentalists. It has always been a source of wonder to me that with Irish music, while everybody else is having a whale of a time, the musicians look as if they're playing at a funeral.

Tralee is Kerry's capital, home to the Festival of Kerry. The jewel in the diadem of the Festival is the 'Rose of Tralee' contest, thought up by some shrewd Kerrymen and women as a last-gasp effort to bring some life into the old town and remind the rest of Ireland, not to mind the world, that Kerry was still there, some-where in the south-west. The big idea was to exploit the popu-larity of the old come-all-ye made famous by the great Irish tenor, Count John McCormack. Mindful of the immortal lyric, 'But 'twas not her beauty alone that won me', this was never to be classed as a mere, reviled 'beauty' contest, so feminist boxes were ticked from the beginning. Intelligence was expected, too. Irish roses arrived from all over the world. I came over myself, in the early days, to compère the contest. I brought my wife along to enjoy the festivities, and her enduring memory is of an evening at the Festival Club. As she sipped delicately at the regulation pint of stout, a local lad approached: 'Excuse me, miss, would you like to dance?' Now, in those days, and perhaps even today, in Ireland, if a fellow asked a girl to dance she was expected to comply, notwithstanding the unattractive aspect of the proposer and the usual smell of drink. It was just not done to refuse, reflecting badly as it did on the chap, with loss of face among his peers.

However, the present Lady Wogan, obviously tainted by exposure to sinful British culture, replied, 'Sorry, not at the moment, thank you.' The young man was thunderstruck. Refused a dance. The shame of it! But he was equal to the situation, all his training in early Irish manhood coming to the fore: 'Ah!' said he, 'sure you're too ould for me anyway.'

18 July 2010

A DIP IN THE NIP

I don't know about this sin-sodden corner of the world, but in Ireland public nudity is illegal. In theory at least, striding proudly around my native country in the buff, apart from scandalising passing grannies and inviting the jeers of hooligans and corner boys, could easily earn you 30 days in the local calaboose.

Hats off, then, to the 200 brave ladies of every age and shape, from all four corners of Erin's Isle, who gathered together this month on a beach in Sligo, in the shadow of Ben Bulben's mighty head, and divested themselves of every last stitch, then hurled themselves into the chilly Atlantic waters.

They call it 'A Dip in the Nip' and they're not doing it to flaunt themselves in front of lascivious eyes, nor to 'moon' the local constabulary, but to raise money for cancer charities. Some of these women have suffered the ravages of the disease themselves, but for all of them it takes nerve and courage, knowing that they'll be filmed and photographed. It's a brave, inspiring sight.

A far cry from the Irish beaches of my youth, where unless you could change into the old togs in a beach hut, or a nearby house, and you fancied a go at the briny, you had to do a quick change right at the water's edge. The seaside resort of Kilkee, in County Clare, had three large rock pools known as the 'Pollock Holes'. The first was for children, the second for ladies, and just beyond that, there was a painted sign on the rocks which stated, 'No Women Beyond This Point'.

You see, the third Pollock Hole was for men, where, if the mood took them, the males dived in starkers. A sight, it was rightly thought, no decent self-respecting woman should see. I thought about that sign as I watched those brave ladies 'dipping in the nip'. Next year they've invited men to strip off and join them. That's what you call 'progress' in Ireland.

Hard to believe, with the lake waters of Lough Erne lapping 'with low sounds by the shore', that the peace of this beautiful, tranquil corner of this island could ever be shattered by violence and bloodshed, but bombs have destroyed people and the lives of their families close to these still waters, in Omagh and Enniskillen.

Despite the recent riots of the marching season, peace has 'come dropping slow' in Northern Ireland. The watchtowers, armed police and soldiers that manned the border crossing points between here and the Republic have been replaced by bureaux de change, where sterling is exchanged for euros, and filling stations on the Republic side, where a steady stream of motorists and lorries from the North refuel more cheaply than they can five minutes down the road on their side. That's also what you call 'progress' in Ireland.

25 July 2010

THE RAINMAKER

I've missed them again, the sunflowers. They were early this year, apparently. As they say in Ireland, 'If it was raining soup, 'twould be a fork I'd have.' As they also say in Ireland, 'I see you've brought the rain with you,' and, inevitably, 'You should have been here yesterday, it was lovely.'

There is a strong feeling among my family and friends that I don't need a headdress, a mask and a grass skirt to be known as 'The Rainmaker', and I'm bound to admit that I appear to be followed around by my own personal moisture-filled mist. I spent two weeks some years ago in what can only be described as damp conditions in Barbados, in the height of the season. Recently, in Ireland, while Britain's grass turned brown 'neath a scorching sun, the rain followed me faithfully from Waterford to Cork, from Kerry to Limerick, as far as Derry and Belfast in the North of Ireland.

And don't talk to me about 'soft' Irish rain. This week I flew into the south-west of France for a mini-break, straight into the worst electrical storm I've ever seen – even here. Sheet lightning, forked lightning, bursts of rain that would have done justice to a monsoon. In the two-minute dash between the airport terminal and the car park, it would have been hard for the passing stranger to distinguish me from a drowned rat. Not that storms are all that unusual down here: every 10 years or so, a big wind blows in off the Bay of Biscay and takes down thousands of trees and, more particularly, the chimney and slates off my roof. They tell me it's the price I pay for peace and quiet. They never told me about the storms when I was buying the house, of course.

I didn't find that out until I visited a French wine shop in London. I remarked on a bottle of Armagnac from a château near my home. 'Ah,' said the helpful assistant, 'Le Gers [the *département* in which I have my simple bothy], *fameux pour les orages.*' Famous for its storms. *Merci.*

Then I comforted myself that it was worth it for the green of the vines, the fields of waving wheat, the blaze of gold as the sunflowers turned their faces to their god. Maybe it was the thought of my imminent arrival, carrying with me the threat, at best, of overcast conditions, but the sunflowers have turned their faces to the ground. Brown, drooping, awaiting their Grim Reaper. Early this year. Great.

If anybody has the immortal gall to say, 'You should have been here last week,' it's goodbye to the *entente cordiale*. And I won't be responsible for my actions if somebody tells me that the weather at home has been great while I've been away.

Oh look, it's starting to rain again. And I haven't even done my dance yet.

8 August 2010

TOO-WIT, TOO-WOO

It's welcome news that sanity has been restored among the burghers of Plymouth city council, and the ban on a pensioner to stop him from taking his pet owls for a walk lifted after a public outcry. The ban was nothing more nor less than a flagrant denial of a Briton's inalienable right to give his animals some bracing exercise, be they furred, feathered or scaled. It's not as if the walking of pet birds is without precedent. Many years ago, I began to receive reports to my radio programme from Solihull, a salubrious suburb of Birmingham, of a man who took his budgie for a daily constitutional around the Robin Hood Roundabout. There he would stand, letting his little feathered friend breathe in the health-giving fumes. Further reports told me that the Man with the Budgie had been perambulating with his caged friend for years, but never on cold, wet days. They told me that the budgie would sing and hop about merrily, giving the lie to the cynical, who claimed it was stuffed . . .

Inevitably, this kindly tale was taken to excess by a listener who claimed that he knew a man who used to take his goldfish for a walk. Naturally, he asserted, this took endless training, starting by taking the fish out of the water for a few seconds, and gradually increasing the time spent out-of-bowl. While this exacting routine was going on, the water in the goldfish bowl was gradually reduced until, in the end, the little fish was completely oxygenised. How this man and his fish would look forward to their daily stroll. Sadly, all too soon, tragedy struck. One day, while crossing a bridge, the goldfish slipped its lead, fell into the river below, and was drowned.

I read with surprise the idea being put forward by some road safety buffs that lines of trees, placed at regular, shrewd intervals along our highways, would have the effect of calming the driver and his vehicle. I say 'surprise', because as every motorist who has ever taken to the roads of France will attest, the tree-lined roads that Napoleon designed to give his troops some shade as they marched seem to have the opposite effect to 'calming' on the average French motorist and lorry driver.

Indeed, a couple of years ago my local *département* in France was seriously considering the demand of a local deputy that roadside trees be cut down. A chap in his constituency, still feeling the effects of the night before, had crashed into a tree while going for his morning baguette, and paid the ultimate penalty. The deputy blamed the tree. If it hadn't been there, he said, the unfortunate driver could have careered into a field of corn or sunflowers, and still be alive to this day . . .

22 August 2010

LAST SUPPERS

Some weeks ago a former senior judicial official in China was executed, having been found guilty of corruption, protecting crime syndicates, and rape. Access was granted to him on death row to two newspaper reporters, who closely observed his final days. Cutting to the chase, what intrigued me was the man's final meal: steamed eggs and a pear. I know Chinese taste buds can be a far cry from our own: one reads of the apparent enjoyment they take from poached sea slugs and duck's feet with a certain reserve, but steamed eggs and a pear for afters for your final feed on this earth? It does seem a little parsimonious on the part of the Chinese prison authorities. Surely they could have stretched the budget to a Peking duck, with the odd noodle, for someone about to breathe his last? But maybe that's the way he wanted it. It might well be that a lightly steamed egg, followed by a juicy ripe pear, were at the very zenith of his earthly delights, although it seems to our Western eyes and tastes a far cry from whoever it was who wanted to pass away 'eating foie gras to the sound of trumpets'. And what happened to the good old judicial principle of 'the condemned man ate a hearty breakfast'?

I'm sure, like myself, you've often pondered what exotic delights with which to stretch the culinary abilities of the prison cooks, before being hung, drawn and quartered. A bit like those lists of musical favourites that everybody makes up in their quieter moments, just in case they're ever asked to appear on *Desert Island Discs*.

Since we no longer enjoy public executions and the death penalty is a thing of the past, I suppose you could say that it's idle speculation, but no more so than your chance of sitting close to Kirsty Young. I'm always disappointed in the final breakfast choice of the condemned in those United States that still believe in the efficacy of 'a life for a life'. They inevitably go for 'a burger and fries, followed by Key lime pie'. Junk. You'd be better off with a steamed egg. And a pear, if you really wanted to be difficult. Myself, I'd insist on an 'Ulster fry', the national dish of Northern Ireland: fried eggs, beans, sausages, bacon, black pudding, white pudding, fried bread and potato bread. And a better than even chance of cheating the hangman with a heart attack.

I can't let this salutary tale go by without telling you the final words of this Chinese man about to meet his end, to his son. That's another thing we old geezers think about: our final words. Will they be courageous, nostalgic, sad, happy or, more importantly, wise? When asked his father's last words, the son replied: 'He told me not to play too many online games'.

I blame the eggs.

29 August 2010

WITS AND WISDOM

The vexed question of whether performers on radio, television, theatre or film are entitled to use their popularity, and perceived influence over their public, to express political or controversial opinions hit the headlines this week. Jason Manford, *The One Show* presenter, sounded off about his opinions on the Government's lack of support for wounded soldiers being edited out by the BBC. Pretty plucky, I'd say, since he has only been in the job a couple of weeks, even though he says his 'proper' job is as a comedian, which he obviously feels gives his opinions the right to be taken seriously. More seriously than those of a television presenter.

Try telling that to Stephen Fry who, this week, has joined a multi-skilled band of protesters to object to the Pope's visit being treated as a State occasion. Fry's opinions on anything and everything are positively revered, in a way that those of, say, Michael Winner never can be. It's different in the States, where every dog and devil who ever showed his face in front of a camera or microphone for 10 seconds is acclaimed a celebrity, whose opinions are sought and freely given on every subject under the sun. The more famous play a very real role in American politics, throwing the weight of themselves and their publicity machines behind their favoured candidates and parties.

Who can forget the posturing of Jane Fonda? Some stars have even gone fully political: Clint Eastwood, Mayor of Carmel; Arnold Schwarzenegger, Governor of California; and Ronald Reagan, President of the United States, for heaven's sake. If Oprah went for the Big Job, she could have it on a plate.

It couldn't happen here, could it? All right, the people of Luton rejected Esther Rantzen, which wouldn't have happened if an American of similar TV status was running for office in Little

Rock, Arkansas. Yet didn't Martin Bell make the transition from reporter to Westminster, and the former hoofer, Betty Boothroyd, become Speaker of the House? I wouldn't discount Stephen Fry's chances if he ever decided to challenge the hustings.

But let's hope that the British public will continue to prefer 'celebs' to keep their opinions to themselves. Certainly the politician who complimented Huw Edwards on never expressing an opinion feels that way. Huw is the consummate professional newsreader, and we must be grateful that he would never, as a Norwegian newsreader did this week, refuse to read the news because 'nothing important has happened'. She quit on the spot, claiming that she could 'now eat properly again, and breathe'.

Huw breathes easily, and feeds well, I'm sure, and can be relied upon to turn up fully dressed – unlike the Slovenian newsreader recently spotted doing national TV news in his underpants. Now, that's not an opinion. That's a statement.

19 September 2010

FOLLOWING THE HERD

I know I'm leaning against the old open door with this, but I've been through a few airports lately, and the general demeanour of the average passenger can only be compared to that of a double agent trying to slip across Checkpoint Charlie in Berlin at the height of the Cold War. It was ever thus, given the cold, cavernous nature of airport terminals, and the inescapable feeling of being herded like sheep from one enclosure to another, without any more information than is vouchsafed to the average sheep.

The general air of doom, gloom and suppressed panic in the traveller's bosom has been enhanced over the past few years with the arrival of 'Security' with a capital 'S'. Only a fool would deny the need for increased vigilance in these parlous times of terrorism; we'd just welcome a little consistency, that's all. Some want your shoes and belt off, others just your shoes, sometimes neither. In Gatwick, they want to measure the size of my hand luggage; in Heathrow, it passes without a murmur. You can leave your mobile phone in the pocket of your jacket in London, you've got to show it in Toulouse – the queues for security in the aforementioned French airport being second only to Dublin in length, and for the same reason: of five security gates, only two are open. An honourable exception is Terminal 5, Heathrow, which had a sticky start but now shows itself to be one of the few in the world built with the weary passenger in mind. Oh, and let's not forget the ritual of the liquids, and any sharp objects. Woe betide those who do not keep their little bottles in a separate transparent bag, and be prepared to be treated like a member of Al-Qaeda if you've forgotten the nail file in your washbag.

And what about the anomaly of 'duty-free'? A listener recounted to me a return trip that he had taken by plane from

America. As he took his seat, he noticed a fellow passenger struggling with his hand luggage, a baseball bat, sealed in a duty-free bag. Not easy to get in an overhead locker. Then another passenger got on, with a large duty-free bottle of whisky. A man on the other side of the plane's aisle was carrying a tennis racket, and then someone else got on, carrying another bottle of something duty-free. During the flight my by now disturbed friend noticed several large bottles of everything from perfume to booze being cheerfully sold from the trolley, all of it over 100ml, the proscribed security limit for dangerous liquids. It crossed my listener's mind that if these people turned out to be terrorists, he might have given them a bit of a fight, if only he hadn't been made to relinquish his bottle of aftershave and his nail scissors at the security check.

26 September 2010

THE CORINTHIAN SPIRIT

With the exception of golf, that most honourable of games – its qualities of decency and sportsmanship epitomised by last weekend's magnificent Ryder Cup – it must be said that sport has lost much of its reputation as an example to the young of the fruits of honest endeavour over the last couple of years.

The 'fixing' of cricket and football matches by shadowy gambling gangs, the cheating with blood capsules in rugby union, the everyday cheating that seems to be part of every football match . . . There's not much 'play up, play up, and play the game' going on – and when you add the drug-enhanced performances of the athletics field, the ridiculous amounts of money paid to even mediocre footballers, the shady dealings of agents and managers, and the avariciousness of club owners (whose only loyalty is to the balance sheet), it paints a depressing picture of the decline of what we used to think of as 'sport'.

All I can say is that it's a far cry from the spirit of *Chariots of Fire*, and men of the calibre of the great Edwardian all-rounder, C.B. Fry, the character of whose exploits on the field of play led to him being offered the kingdom of Albania. He declined, of course. No cricket in Albania, and precious little grouse-shooting.

It's not without its own significance that the only other Briton to whom the crown of Albania might legitimately have been offered was the late and much lamented Norman Wisdom, whose stature in that country was that of a deity. I loved Norman. Every time we met he would pretend to trip over and then crash into me, with that manic laugh. Talk about life imitating art. It can't be more than a couple of years ago that he was still making an audience laugh at an *Oldie* lunch. Chaplin thought him his natural successor, the plucky little tramp. Anyone further removed from

C.B. Fry would be hard to imagine. I seem to have digressed in memory of dear old Norman.

To return to my main thrust: what's happened to the Corinthian spirit, the glory of just taking part? Athletes complaining in Delhi of beetles in the swimming pool, uneven surfaces on the track? What about Lord Burghley training for the Olympic high hurdles with a glass of champagne on each hurdle; Irish rugby internationals, having tied their boots with hairy twine, stubbing out the last cigarette before running out to give their all; Corinthian-Casuals trotting out at Wembley to play Arsenal in the Cup Final, in tennis shirts, their hands in the pockets of their capacious khaki shorts?

Oh, I know the young limbs among you will have me down as a right old curmudgeon, hankering after glory days that only ever existed in the memory; one of those old blokes in a dusty blazer with an obscure club crest, grey flannel trousers and scuffed suede shoes that we used to call 'Alickadoos' – but something great has been lost. Now, where did I put my drink?

10 October 2010

PLAY UP, PLAY UP

I'm not much for beating anything, even a good thing, to death, but to return to my well-meaning, if tedious, rant of last week on the sad passing of sport and sportsmanship, scarcely had the ink dried on my quill before glorious evidence to the contrary paraded itself before me.

Last Saturday, in bracing Reading, Berkshire, I watched a thrilling Heineken European Cup rugby match between my club, London Irish, and the Irish province Munster. My club are known as the 'Exiles', because many are exiled from the Pacific Islands and the Antipodes. Munster is where my emotional rugby heart lies, having been born in Limerick, where, in Thomond Park, resides Irish rugby's very soul. Talk about being 'torn between two lovers'. Munster's followers had come in their thousands, from the furthest corners of Cork and Limerick, to be met by even more thousands of London Irish fans.

Both wore their team's favours and jerseys, waved their scarves, chanted their songs and loudly banged their drums. They did this shoulder to shoulder in the stands, with no bad language, no aggressive behaviour, not a hint of fisticuffs, in front of a barely discernible security presence. They even kept a respectful silence during opponents' penalty kicks. And make no mistake, these rugby followers are every bit as tough and fanatical as their football counterparts. It's a much more physical game, and this one epitomised it. There was hard running, ferocious, back-breaking tackling, almost savage rucking, barely controlled physical mayhem, but nobody cursed or even argued with the referee. Nobody pretended to be hurt, nobody tore off their shirt and ran around like an eejit when they'd scored. At the end of the game the teams shook hands. As the fans streamed home, there was no triumphalism, no bad losers, just people who'd come to support their team.

I returned to Limerick a couple of years ago for a dinner they said was to honour me. A former school rugby team-mate stood to deliver my valedictory address: 'Wogan', he said, 'was a prop, but his heart was at fullback. Certainly, it was in that position he was most frequently to be seen, when things got rough up front. And he found himself in that position, the last line of defence, when our opponents' big lock forward broke through and surged towards our try-line. Only Wogan stood between him and a certain score! Wogan had two alternatives: crash-tackle the huge fellow, or stand aside. Wogan stood aside.'

Heatedly, I denied this as a foul calumny. And I can certainly assert that I never said to the big fella as he passed: 'Good luck with the conversion.'

17 October 2010

AGE AND BEAUTY

And so, the endless whingeing and moaning over 'ageism' in the BBC drones on, alleviated only by the glad news of the Great Engagement, and the painful dismemberment of a poor soul lured to a near-death experience on *I'm a Celebrity, Get Me Out of Here*. An arachnophobic, apparently she didn't expect creepy-crawlies and spiders to turn up in the middle of an Australian rainforest. Not to mention Lembit Öpik who, I recall, once pushed his way into my commentary box at a Eurovision Song Contest to tell me to 'take it easy on Latvia'. The perils of the jungle.

Still, Kate and William and Ant and Dec appear to have, probably only for the moment, pushed ageism at the BBC to the sidelines and letters pages. About time. Apart from the fact that BBC TV and Radio teems with old geezers and gals who would have been pushed out to pasture years ago in any other trade, myself included, we are freelance broadcasters.

It's not a permanent, pensionable position, for goodness' sake. If I'd wanted that, I would have continued separating half-crowns from florins and dirty pound notes from clean in the basement of the Royal Bank of Ireland, Cattle Market branch, Dublin. And I'd be well retired by now.

Years ago, the most popular presenter of his era, the late, great Eamonn Andrews, took a fresh-faced, innocent eejit of a fellow Irishman aside to tell him some home truths about the business into which the little chap had stumbled more by luck than judgement. The three most important things about losing your job in TV and Radio, according to Eamonn, were: 1) the public get tired looking at and listening to you; 2) you get tired doing it; 3) by far the most crucial factor: them on the sixth floor think it's time for you to fold your tent, clear your desk and silently, without fuss, steal away.

You'll notice that the third element has no bearing on the first two, and is the subjective opinion of people who think that they know better than the public.

But that's the game, the risk you take when you decide to stick your face and voice in front of a camera or a microphone, hoping that the public, and the people upstairs, take to you. You chance it that a six-week contract will be extended, and move your family across from security in Ireland on the strength of it.

There is no security in such a life: you have to build your own, taking the brickbats and the failures that are part and parcel of every career in a business without any discernible path, ladder, safety net or permanency. Along with the added risk to your livelihood of the whims and fancies of those in authority over you. So, they think you're too old. It's so unfair. But like that poor woman in the jungle who wasn't expecting spiders, what are you doing here?

21 November 2010

THEY NEVER FORGET

My heart went out, as every right-thinking person's must have, to our poor benighted judges, on the latest austerity measure handed down by the Lord Chief Justice. In future, he's travelling second-class on the train, and has urged his minions to exercise a 'self-denying ordinance' and do likewise.

Putting aside the consideration that 'self-denial' is something you'd rather do on your own than have shoved down your neck, I confess to a fellow-feeling sympathy for my judicial betters. When but a fresh-faced lad, newly arrived on Blighty's shore, I was thrilled to be asked to present *Come Dancing* for BBC Television. While not enjoying the fanatical following that *Strictly* commands now, the show had a loyal and numerous audience that delighted in the brevity of the frocks in the Latin American dances, and the rigorous formality of formation dancing, sadly overlooked by *Strictly* . . .

I was eager to strut my stuff in Mecca and Locarno ballrooms, far flung as they were, from Swansea to Glasgow. Only when I looked at the contract did I reflect, as the good judges must have, following the Lord Chief Justice's stern advice, on the travel arrangements. For it appeared that while the show's producer and director were vouchsafed a first-class rail ticket by the BBC, the talent, or hobbledehoy (me) was to travel steerage. Pluckily, I demurred. The BBC seemed taken aback, but agreed to advance the extra, probably because the incumbent presenter, Peter West, was up to his pads in cricket commentary and couldn't find time to travel. Peter had, at any rate, blotted his copybook in Glasgow the previous year, when an irate audience of ballroom dance lovers had stormed the stage and threatened his life because their team had been defeated. It hardly seemed fair, since Peter was only the presenter, but those were dangerous days on the ballroom floor.

One can only hazard a guess at the grisly fate of Bruno Tonioli, Len Goodman and Craig Revel Horwood, had they been around Sauchiehall Street in those days. And Brucie would never have made it out alive.

I went on to present seven seasons of the show, ranging the countryside in pursuit of spangled excellence, enjoying the sequinned spectaculars, all sewn on by the ladies themselves. Like them, their partners, each bearing a rictus smile, were amateurs, treading the measure fresh from their day jobs. I left feeling I had drained the cup to the lees, and such was the impact I made that after seven years it seemed that most viewers were convinced the show was still being presented by Peter West.

Roll on a decade or two, and blow me down if they don't revive the old warhorse with 'Strictly' in front to show the difference. But do they ask me to present it? Of course not. Long memories at the BBC: they hadn't forgotten my fuss over the rail fare.

28 November 2010

THE KENT COUNTRYSIDE

As we stagger on towards the season of goodwill, from no room in our prisons to no room at the inn, from global warming to freezing, from economic to traffic chaos, from Wiki to Widdy, it should come as no surprise that the editors of otherwise mainly sensible newspapers, drained of all emotion by an endless barrage of bad news, should grasp like giggling schoolchildren at a little light relief.

And joy of joys! It's not only the favourite whipping boy, the BBC, but also Radio 4, and to dust the mince pie with even more sugar, steady Jim Naughtie providing the sniggers. The cup completely overran when Andrew Marr did it again – and all over Jeremy Hunt, the Culture Secretary. Pictures of shamefaced Naughtie graced the front pages, while on Channel 4 News Jon Snow added the comment: 'Spooner or Freud?' Meanwhile, throughout the Hogwarts-land that is television and radio, every presenter who ever took his chances in front of a microphone or camera looked heavenwards and thanked God that it was someone else . . .

Early in a broadcaster's career, the pitfalls are made clear by wiser heads with a simple example of how just one phrase, innocently mangled, can have you out the door, P45 in hand. 'The Kent countryside' is the shining example of a minefield bristling with danger. Approach it at your peril, unless privately wealthy. I'm not sure if even the great Sir Trevor McDonald didn't come a cropper over it.

It's not just old Spooner and Sigmund that you have to tiptoe around; traps lie everywhere. The late Bernard Matthews liked to do his own commercials, and couldn't understand why the advertising agency was aghast at his loudly declaimed slogan: 'Try my turkeys. They're Norfolk and good!' Say it quickly and you'll see why.

A radio presenter in Ireland, in a two-way link with Australia, was discussing the merits of the songbird Kylie Minogue. The Australian wanted to talk about Kylie's attributes other than her voice: 'She's got great legs!' The Irish presenter, a lady, replied primly: 'But legs apart, what do you think of her?'

As a boy broadcaster I presented an Irish radio show called *Hospital Requests*. TB being rampant at the time, the idea was to cheer the many people in hospital with music requested by their family and friends. Realising that if I kept slavishly to the public choice I'd play nothing but Count John McCormack and Fr Sydney MacEwan, I would occasionally introduce a new song. The Clancy Brothers were enormously popular, and I'd got their latest, 'Isn't it grand, boys?', just before I went on air. Perfect to cheer the ailing. Shame I didn't listen to it before I played it. 'Isn't it grand, boys' was followed by 'to be bloody well dead!'

I can laugh about it now . . . and so will you, Jim, some day.

12 December 2010

VERY LITTLE DOES ME . . .

'Very little for me, now. A slice of breast and a little brown meat, just a spoonful of stuffing, oh, and that's too much gravy. Is that ham? Goodness, no . . . a half-potato, then, and that small Brussels sprout. Can you cut that chipolata in half for me? I'll never drink all that wine, is there any fizzy water? I had a slice of smoked salmon to start; I'm not able for any more. I probably won't finish all of this . . .'

How I wish that had been me yesterday, as I steer clear of the weighing scales, knowing that I still won't be able to control myself in front of today's roast beef. That earlier rant was my Auntie Nellie, in long-gone days in Dublin, around the kitchen table at the granny's for Christmas Day. 'Very little does me' was my Auntie Nellie's watchword whenever food was placed in front of her, and, like many people who regard themselves as abstemious to a fault, she was as round as a barrel of bread-soda. She only picked at her food, but that was on a 12-hour daily basis.

There wasn't much of the spirit of Christmas past, as epitomised by dear old Aunt Nell, around our groaning board yesterday. It was more like a Tudor romp, with yours truly in the role of Henry VIII, as portrayed by Charles Laughton. I'm not saying that I was chucking turkey bones over my shoulder, and grabbing a handful of the nearest serving wench. No, the bones remained stripped naked on the plate, and wives seem to draw the line at being grabbed over the gravy these days.

Actually, enough of the braggadocio; I'm not the man I was around the turkey and his trimmings. Gone are the days when our hero could be found prostrate on the dining room floor, pole-axed by that last lump of stuffing and turkey skin. (It's a digression, but would turkey be worth tuppence, if it wasn't for the skin? And that goes for goose, only more so. Goose is all brown meat, and there's not enough of it. Honestly, Nigella, you'd have been better off with a chicken.)

And this near-catatonic state would have happened long before anybody even mentioned the pudding – not that anybody mentions the pudding in this neck of the woods, even in these days of a slightly less stuffed father of the feast. We didn't even consider Heston's Orange in a Pond thing. All my family ever aspired to on Christmas Day was getting past the Big Bird. We never troubled ourselves with charades, board games or cards. We just sprawled there, until it was time for the turkey and stuffing sandwiches. (And it had better be white bread. We're not at war.)

Now all is changed, changed utterly. There are little people around again, all is noise and excitement, and a grandpa had better be on his toes, stuffed or not . . . And don't tell me 'batteries not included'.

26 December 2010

A FRENCHMAN'S HOME

Here, in south-west France, the shutters in every village house are firmly closed. It's nothing new; the same shutters are firmly closed in the summer as well. Many think it's to keep the heat in during the winter and out in the summer. I'm not so sure. An Englishman's home is his castle, and so is a Frenchman's, except that his has the drawbridge up, permanently. In this rural, remote region, the Gascon guards his privacy and his land fiercely. French farm dogs are not trained to nuzzle up affectionately to the stranger; *au contraire*, approach one only in full body armour, and the same goes for the dog's owner.

Some years ago, a friend, a guest at our son's wedding here in France, got my inadequate directions wrong, and drove his car through the entrance of another house. The farmer was out in an instant. Our friend, realising he was in the wrong place, wound down his car window to apologise and was immediately punched in the face.

Out of curiosity, I have walked into a field to have a look at a tumbledown property, and found myself threatened physically by the owner who came roaring up behind me, demanding to know my business there. Lately, not far from here, a farmer shot dead another who, he claimed, was stealing his truffles.

And yet, these *agricoles*, the very salt of the earth of France, across whose darkened thresholds you are unlikely ever to be asked, throw fêtes and *foires*, carnivals and circuses in every town, village and hamlet, and every passing stranger is welcome to try his luck with the gizzards, garlic and snails.

We live close to the *chemins*, the routes taken by pilgrims from all over Europe for a thousand years, following the foothills of the Pyrenees to Santiago de Compostela in northern Spain. Their emblem is a scallop shell, hence the 'coquille St Jacques'.

However, another pilgrimage, based on the predictions of the extinct Mayan people of South America, is taking place even now, in the hills east of the Pyrenees. There, an outcrop of rock, the Pic de Bugarach, is believed to have been assigned by extra-terrestrials as a place to survive the Armageddon predicted by the Mayans: 21 December 2012. Hundreds of New Age pilgrims have already set up homes there because time is short, and you don't want to miss getting a seat in the spacecraft that lies under the mountain.

Given that there are enough numpties out there who not only want to believe this extraterrestrial tosh, but also the predictions of a sun-worshipping, blood-sacrificing, long-extinct, pagan tribe, the mayor of the little village of Bugarach rightly fears being overrun by sandals, beards and backpacks for the next couple of years.

He wants to call in the military; there are simply not enough farm dogs. And guess who won't be welcome at the Bugarach fête this year?

9 January 2011

THE PHOENIX

I hope you'll join me for the first part of *Terry Wogan's Ireland*, tonight on BBC One. The word 'journey' has become as abused as 'celebrity', so if it's all the same to you, I'd rather you treated it as more of a meander, a dawdle.

It's a big little island, and we haven't done more than skim the surface in two one-hour shows, but I have enough memories for a lifetime: the boatman, Michael, insisting on making us tea as we wallowed on a mercifully calm Atlantic, in the shadow of the great Fastnet Lighthouse; and Enniskerry, one of Ireland's prettiest villages, in the lovely Wicklow Mountains, where my father was born. He left at 15, on the basis that 'you couldn't eat the scenery'.

My father was the great-grandson of Michael Wogan, the village bootmaker, pictured in 1901 with a beard like a herbaceous border. Old Michael is seen with Lord Powerscourt, with matching beard, and others of his Lordship's loyal serfs on his estate. Powerscourt has now been restored to its glory, with beautiful Italianate gardens and, at the front of the house, the sunken road that his Lordship made so that he and his good Lady might be spared the sight of his servants coming to work.

I took in the lovely little harbours, Portmagee and Baltimore, a delight to the eye and the spirit; the honeysuckle and fuchsia hedges of Clear Island; the grandeur of Killarney's lakes, even more dramatic when shrouded in dark clouds; the swans on the River Shannon at Limerick, and the little house where I spent my first 15 years. I'm on this 'journey' to see how Ireland has changed. The biggest change of all is crossing the border between the Republic and Northern Ireland. Where once there were watch-towers, checkpoints and armed soldiers, there are open roads and bureaux de change where the euro can be changed for the pound. The only clue that you've crossed the border is when the road signs change from kilometres to miles. Of course, in Northern Ireland old prejudices die hard, and it's not so much the side of the tracks on which you were born, but which side of the river. The River Boyne was where William of Orange defeated the Jacobites. Hundreds of years later, they still march to the drums in Northern Ireland to celebrate the Protestant victory.

The Ireland I left in the sixties was a poor place, cursed by emigration. By the nineties it was booming, the most successful country in Europe. The Celtic Tiger roared and the Irish, who'd never experienced anything like it before, lived the dream. We know that it all fell apart, but these people and this island have a history that puts the present into perspective.

As I hope these two films will show, there's still laughter here, and music, a joy of life and living. How can anyone think that the Irish will not rise again?

23 January 2011

THE IRON LADY

Meryl Streep's resemblance to Margaret Thatcher, in a still photo taken on the set of *The Iron Lady*, the film based on the Lady's political career, is almost frightening. The bouffant hair, the wide eyes with their intimidating stare, the half-open mouth with its bold red lipstick. Even the gap in the front teeth; it's Maggie, to the life. It must have sent frissons of fear through the corridors of Brussels and Strasbourg. No doubt the greatest screen actress of her generation will bring Thatcher to blinding life, but does she really have to look so much like her?

Take a brief look at some of the rest of the cast: Jim Broadbent looks nothing like Denis Thatcher, Olivia Colman doesn't come even close to resembling daughter Carol, and if they can get Richard E. Grant vaguely to approximate Michael Heseltine, it'll be a miracle of prosthetics. The two younger actors who are to play the roles of Margaret and Denis as young man and woman will get away with it, because we've little or no idea what our hero and heroine looked like when young. Indeed, it's hard to imagine.

It's the principle on which Madame Tussauds has been getting away with murder for years. Jack the Ripper, Elizabeth I, Henry VIII – all those historical figures seem so lifelike because we have no idea what they really looked like. As soon as the waxworks stray into modernity, we can see that they look nothing like the real McCoy.

What you make of Helena Bonham Carter as a young Queen Mum, Colin Firth in *The King's Speech* looks nothing like the King George we see in photos and old newsreels, but he didn't have to. The acting was good enough, just as it was for Helen Mirren as the Queen. I just hope that Meryl Streep didn't go to all the bother of having that front tooth removed specially for the role.

I've been privileged to meet Lady Thatcher on a few occasions.

Two that spring to mind: at Rye golf course, Denis had finished his round and was enjoying a tipple in the club bar when Margaret arrived to collect him. Ladies weren't allowed in the bar, so the Prime Minister sat meekly in another little room, on her own, until Denis was ready to leave. I interviewed herself for television, and she and Denis joined us afterwards for the famous BBC cocktail sausages in peanut sauce and red or white wine of doubtful provenance. They even opened the spirits cabinet. Well, she was Prime Minister, after all.

The Lady was charm itself, belying her by now fearsome reputation. Denis was enjoying himself hugely, fulminating on 'pinkoes' in the BBC, while putting away the G&Ts. He was certainly on his fourth, and reaching for another, when The Lady Who Was Not For Turning, but who'd been watching and listening closely, turned and said, 'Denis! That's your second! We must be off.'

13 February 2011

JAMBO!

My visit to East Africa included a trip to the Masai Mara, where I saw enough zebras, giraffes, monkeys, mongooses, gazelles, elephants, lions and hyenas to last me a lifetime. And Italians. All Kenya seemed alive with them, and nobody could tell me why. You never see Italian tourists in Spain, France or anywhere else, apart from Oxford Street. So how come the beaches and the bush of Africa have an Italian beneath every umbrella, behind every tree? There must be money in this for some university research study, if they can tear themselves away from frightening us off beef.

'Jambo is the greeting you will get, just west of Zanzibar' – a popular song from a fifties movie, and as true today as it ever was. Cheerful folk greet strangers with a smiling 'Jambo!' and, if you don't respond immediately and in kind, they follow up with, 'Hakunah matata!' Frankly, at first, to the inhibited ear it's an embarrassment, an encounter you'd rather have avoided, like the person who sits beside you on a plane and strikes up a conversation that may have to be sustained for hours, or that ultimate pariah, the man who wants to talk in a lift, when all any right-thinking person wants to do is look straight ahead until it's time to get out again. Of course, after a couple of days of greetings the social restrictions imposed by Western urban living dissipate, and you're 'Jamboing' like a good 'un.

I must confess, however, to the unworthy suspicion that life may be imitating art here. Did anybody in East Africa say 'Jambo' before that fifties movie? I have more doubts about 'Hakunah matata', translated as 'No worries'. This phrase is part of the lyrics of a song from *The Lion King*, written by Sir Tim Rice, and, if I may speak frankly, I think he made it up. And as with 'Jambo', it caught on with the locals and is indistinguishable from their language and folklore now. How do we know what these words mean? They could just as easily be translated as, say, 'That man is a witch doctor. He has a frog in his pocket!'

Just in case you think you're dealing with a cynical numpty here – while not claiming to be an expert in Swahili, many years ago a radio listener sent me some telling Swahili phrases, which, sadly, I had little opportunity to use. For instance, the following, with rough translation: 'Mavi haya ya lini?'('How old are these droppings?'), or 'Nimuemwa na nyoka' ('That snake has bitten me'). But this one may come in handy if you're thinking of a safari: 'Watapata katuona kutoka hapa?' ('Can they smell us from here?')

13 March 2011

A GRAND DAY OUT

I don't know whether, given the parlous state of Ireland's economy, fewer Irish punters than usual made their annual pilgrimage to Cheltenham for the great National Hunt Festival meeting – but those that did seemed to be kicking up as much of a racket as usual. And Irish trainers and jockeys seemed to be enjoying their success, helping their fellow countrymen do their bit to reduce the National Debt.

Years ago, when I was a boy broadcaster, the BBC, in a moment of weakness, sent me on St Patrick's Day to present the radio coverage of the festival. You will appreciate the demented logic that inspired the choice; after all, what could be more appropriate than to send an Irishman to cover an occasion which the Irish have regarded as their own since they kidnapped St Patrick at a point-to-point in North Wales? The problem was that I know as much about horses and racing as I do about snipe-shooting. It's assumed that an Irishman's best friend is his horse, but for me, and a million urban Irishmen like me, the horse is an unpredictable animal with teeth and a kick. I've been on more elephants than I have horses.

It can be chilly on the plains of Cheltenham, a wind that comes down the hill faster than the horses. On that memorable St Patrick's Day, a vicious shower of spring sleet seemed to blow from the ground up, straight into the very nostrils. We Wogans are oft compared to the Inuit for our resistance to icy conditions, but I confess to the odd shiver, as the wind pierced my corrugated-iron underwear as though it were chiffon.

I soldiered on through chattering teeth until the Big One, the Gold Cup. It was won by a horse named Alverton, English-owned and Yorkshire-trained, but ridden by a jockey from County Cork, the legendary Jonjo O'Neill. Now, one of the reasons why the

Irish love Cheltenham is because they can really let their hair down and behave in a manner that they'd never get away with at home on the Curragh, or even Limerick Junction.

So there we were, Jonjo and me, in the unsaddling enclosure, live on the radio, as the great man described how the race had run and been won, when one of our whooping fellow countrymen leapt over the rails, rushed up to Jonjo, threw his arms around him and screeched, 'Jonjo, you're a hooer!' In certain parts of Ireland, 'whore', pronounced 'hooer', is taken to be a high compliment, meaning a shrewd rascal, a right rogue.

What a few million British BBC radio listeners made of it is not recorded. If 'compliance' had been around then, I might never have been heard of again.

20 March 2011

A FEW BALLS SHORT . . .

Many years ago, before the world went mad and it wasn't so easy to mastermind computer attacks on the CIA and become a 'cyber terrorist' without ever leaving your bedroom, the mail from the listeners to my morning radio show was exclusively by card or letter – 'snail mail', as those on the cutting edge of technology call it.

Often I could tell the state of mind of my correspondents not just by the eccentricity of their writings, but by the writing itself. The more eccentric, not to say crazy, the theme of the letter, the more wayward the script. I remarked upon this once to someone P.G. Wodehouse would describe as 'a loony doctor', and told him that it seemed to me that a good 20 per cent of the population were, to a greater or lesser extent, not the full shilling. 'It's more like thirty-three and a third per cent!' he said, with a merry laugh. Ever afterwards, I have found myself walking the streets of London with a wary eye on my fellow pedestrians, looking for their quirks and tics. And I'm here to tell you that, although my observational sample may be wrong again, I don't think the 'loony doctor' was a million miles off the mark.

So, how to spot someone who appears, more than the rest of us, round the twist, and whom we'd be well advised to cross to the other pavement to avoid? Not that you could do that safely in London, with all the buses and the holes in the road; you'd just have to make a quick decision on which option was the more life-threatening. I read that there is a test, designed by another loony doctor – all right, psychologist – that provides some simple tests that the man on the pavement, or avoiding death in the street, can readily apply. Your psychopath, apparently, is glib, with a grandiose sense of self-worth, prone to boredom, cunning, shallow, impulsive, parasitic, irresponsible and promiscuous. Or maybe they just work in television . . .

Wimbledon fortnight provides the keen observer of mild eccentricity with plenty of examples among the greats of the tennis world. I'm sure that they don't know they're doing it, but there are clear indications of Obsessive Compulsive Disorder to delight the amateur psychologist everywhere you look, particularly on the Centre Court. The screaming of Sharapova, Azarenka and Schiavone, Djokovic's incessant ball-bouncing before serving, Roddick's adjustment of crotch and shirt after every rally, and the greatest of them all, Nadal, placing his bags and his water bottles just so, and continually pulling at his underpants. I'm waiting for Rory McIlroy to tell us that he can only play golf after he's had an Ulster Fry for breakfast, and a change of shirt on the 10th tee.

26 June 2011

SUITED AND BOOTED

On high days and holidays, birthdays and anniversaries, such as today is for herself and yours truly (46 years ago, Rathmines parish church, Dublin, in the rain, in case anyone's lost count) the present Lady Wogan and myself tend to throw caution to the wind, with little or no regard for the parlous state of the economy, and treat ourselves to what the comic papers of our era called 'a slap-up meal'. Remember? Desperate Dan's was a huge cow pie, with horns, cooked by his Aunt Aggie. Lord Snooty smacked his lips at sausage and mash, a great mountain of potato with two giant sausages sticking out like the horns on the aforementioned cow pie.

Nowadays, if Gregg Wallace of *Masterchef* is to be believed, what we should be searching for is 'a nice plate of food'. That's what the good lady and myself are after, and it's not pie and mash with a side order of jellied eels. As the mighty Gregg puts it so well, we go for 'top-end dining'.

We get dressed up for our treat, she in a smart little something that she's had for years (but I've never seen before) and myself in shirt, suit and tie, with pocket handkerchief, as worn. Formally but correctly dressed, and looking forward to an evening of high delight: it's the way we've always done it, it's the way it always used to be done. Even as we are led to our table by an attentive maître d', however, it becomes clear that while we're done up to the nines, many of the rest of the clientele of this three-Michelin-star restaurant look as if they've just jogged in from the gym. Pullovers, jeans, tennis shoes. Doesn't anywhere maintain a dress code any more? These people would be better off in a Chicago speakeasy.

It's the inverted snobbery that gets me: the jeans, the scuffed shoes are shrieking, 'Look at me, I dress how I like, where I like.

Take me as you find me. I eat in places like this all the time. Loadsa money!'

Gordon Brown pulled a 'man o' the people' act a couple of years ago when he refused to wear black tie at a City dinner. I'd always given the present Prime Minister credit for a bit more sense, and then he tried his ridiculous 'economy flight to Malaga' stunt. I put it down to a momentary lapse, and then he blew it all away by declaring that he'd be wearing a lounge suit for The Wedding. Our Prime Minister – surrounded by the royal family in their formal gowns, uniforms, jewels, diadems and decorations, the crowned heads of Europe similarly caparisoned, and everybody else in at least a morning suit with tails – striking a blow for the common man, in a lounge suit.

And then, when all hope is gone, common sense overtakes the common man. We can only hope and pray that Moss Bros still has one left on the rail that fits him.

24 April 2011

PLUM LINES

At the moment, I'm up to my shoulder pads in a documentary for BBC Two on one of my literary idols, P.G. Wodehouse. Better men than I have idolised the great Plum, among them George Orwell, Evelyn Waugh and Hilaire Belloc, who thought Wodehouse 'the best writer of English now alive'. One of the best ever, I'd say, and anybody who loves the English language would have a hard time disagreeing.

However, the problem with a concentrated dose of the great man's writings is the marked tendency that goes with it of boring family, friends and passing strangers with PG's brilliant turn of phrase, blinding similes, not to mention the classical and scriptural allusions. I find that once I start, everyone else has got their favourite Wodehouseism as well. Stephen Fry, who played Jeeves to Hugh Laurie's Bertie Wooster in that marvellous television series of a few years ago, quotes the old boy brilliantly. One of his favourites is the description of a would-be dictator as having 'the sort of eye that can open an oyster at 60 paces'. I have a fondness for: 'He looked like a Bishop who has just discovered schism and doubt among the minor clergy.'

But don't get me started. I wouldn't have mentioned it at all, except for a nugget I turned up in a popular daily the other day – the same newspaper that keeps me abreast of the latest 'miracle' fruit or vegetable that will keep all of us alive for ever, as if the NHS wasn't in enough trouble, and vital information on pain-free body waxing, as well as the boon to your sex life that chocolate-covered strawberries can bring.

This particular newsworthy nosegay was on the subject of names, and how we all enjoy endless hours of innocent pleasure from jeering the ridiculous first names with which celebrity chefs, film stars and pop idols lumber their children, thereby ensuring .

that the unfortunate kids are marked for life by the sneering and bullying they have to endure in their schooldays. It turns out that irresponsible naming of offspring by besotted parents is nothing new. Victorians and Edwardians sprayed foolish names about like Christmas Day at the workhouse: Koko, for instance. And Egremont, Arcissadella and Eustacia.

In the Ireland of my youth, there was a tendency among the more pious to name the little ones after obscure saints. I knew an Athanasius and a Berchmans. Although I'm not sure if the current fashion for the secular is an improvement. Kylie, Elvis, Madonna and Clint don't sit any more easily on Irish surnames . . .

As I say, it would have passed me by as the idle wind, if it hadn't put me in mind of perhaps my all-time favourite Wodehouse bon mot: 'There's some raw work done at the baptismal font, Jeeves.'

3 July 2011

LIQUID ASSETS

Even as I write, the United States teeters on the brink of defaulting on its national debt, and Barack Obama interrupts television schedules to plead for the right to print more money; Britain is barely keeping its economic head above water; the eurozone is banjaxed; and someone has just bought a bottle of wine for £75,000.

It's 200 years old, but he's not going to drink it for another six years. After such a long time, I suppose another few years is neither here nor there, but how can this certifiable chump bear the temptation of just looking at the bottle, without succumbing to the urge to open it? The last time it was tasted, 12 years ago, it was described as 'liquefied crème brûlée'. Pausing only to say that if I'm served a watery crème brûlée, I send it back, it's undeniable that, to the oenophile, the bottle of Château d'Yquem 1811 will have an almost sacred significance. But it's hardly a work of art that you can proudly exhibit to your friends, like a Turner or a Freud. For how long can you sit and admire a bottle?

Well, according to the new owner, he will install it 'amid Fort Knox security', for diners to slaver over, in his restaurant in Bali. Bali? Tropical haven of sunshine and grass skirts it may be, but I've never heard of anybody going there for haute cuisine and fine wines. This man is taking an extraordinary risk. How does he know it will travel? How many times has the steady wine drinker here been told that certain varieties of the grape can't even make the journey across the Channel without suffering grievous harm? What am I saying? He'll be lucky if he can get the cork out before it crumbles in a thousand pieces into his bottle of liquid gold.

It will be a stressful evening in 2017 when this man celebrates with his family at La Tour d'Argent in Paris, as the timeless Seine flows by.

Ah, La Tour d'Argent . . . Never been there, but the present wife has. Years ago, when the world was young, and the pair of us ditto, herself took on a modelling engagement in Paris with the House of Balmain, leaving me to my own devices in Dublin. She flew back one weekend, and we went out to dinner. After excited descriptions of life in the great fashion house, and the social whirl of the Left Bank and the boulevards, I quizzed her closely on my main interest: the restaurants.

Almost airily, she said she'd particularly liked the ambience of La Tour d'Argent. I could hardly control myself. 'Tell me all,' I cried, 'sparing not the smallest detail of the meal!' And, showing off my knowledge of the dish for which La Tour was far famed, I asked:

'And the *canard pressé*, the pressed duck, how was it?'

'Oh,' said my good Catholic girl, 'it was a Friday. I had the fish.'

Funny, the conversations you never forget . . .

31 July 2011

SUPERSONIC

Last Monday found me comfortably ensconced in the 'Concorde' lounge of Terminal 5, Heathrow airport, thanks to the kindly ministrations of British Airways gentlefolk. Sitting there, I was reminded of the glory days of Concorde itself, and what a loss to the well-to-do and urgent traveller, and this country's prestige, was the demise of this magnificent piece of engineering.

It's as if we've gone backwards – but then we appear to be retreating on so many fronts lately that the loss of an aeroplane means little or nothing in the chaos of economic meltdown and the breakdown of social order. Still, I have my memories of Concorde: breakfast at Heathrow, and breakfast again on arrival in New York; the darkness of the ionosphere as we flew high above the surly bounds of earth; the gentle lurch forward as the sound barrier was breached.

I presented a radio programme to celebrate the inaugural flight to Singapore, reporting from Bahrain, where we paused to catch our breath, then Singapore where I had a couple of hours before heading home on Concorde once more. I noticed that the plane had 'British Airways' on one side, 'Singapore Airlines' on the other. During its brief stay on the Tarmac it was noticeable that only the Singapore Airlines side had been cleaned – which was always the problem with Concorde.

I well remember on that flight that we were forbidden to fly over some countries' airspace. There can have been no good reason other than envy. The Americans were, at first, reluctant to allow Concorde to put down anywhere on the Land of the Free, but bowed eventually to the inevitable, probably under pressure from David Frost, who couldn't have pursued his dazzling dual television career between New York and London without it.

My last trip on the great supersonic bird was as a steward, on the Washington flight. It was part of a series I was doing for BBC Radio 4 called *The Day Job* – our hero as barman, serviceman and other daily grinds – over which time has drawn a merciful veil. I took the customers' coats, poured champagne, dished up canapés and hid in the galley from a demanding grande dame.

My mellow lounge mood disappeared as I read an interview I'd given to publicise Proms in the Park, in September. It hardly got a mention. I'll never learn. It's the same with golf; 40 years on, I'm still lifting my head.

14 August 2011

FAIR PLAY

The shutters and doors are closed, as the villages and hamlets of rural France return to their timeless silence. A dog barks, a faraway machine gathers the grapes, but no human voice is heard. The 'far fierce hour and sweet' of the fairs, hosted by every little handful of houses here for a couple of glorious days in August, is over. For those frantic days, the deserted villages of France come to life.

People appear out of nowhere in their hundreds to sing and dance, eat, drink and be merry. We do our best in Britain with the yearly hog roast, but it's a tame, respectable affair, with everybody tucked up in bed well before midnight. The village fête is a French tradition, and they go for it in their time-honoured way: a bar is set up, a band plays loud French pop (as the discerning Eurovision viewer will know, it's a musical form that they've never really mastered – should have stuck with the accordion) and the dancing goes on until the wee small hours. There's no drunkenness, the young men and women mix happily with their elders, it's companionable and friendly, and nobody gives a Continental hoot that the roast lamb is served a good hour after the first course, melon and ham. The wine is plentiful, and there's apple tart and ice cream to follow. Since it costs all of about 14 quid a head, it seems churlish to complain about a little delay.

And if the prospect of boring old roast lamb fails to titillate your jaded palate, there are other delights on offer elsewhere. There's the *demoiselles*, for instance. The French get their monies' worth out of the duck: liver, leg, breast, wing, heart and gizzard. For the *demoiselles* they roast the only bits left: the bones. I know people who even claim to have found meat. This year, I signed up for an *escargolade*, a snail marathon. No, not an interminable race for slow-moving molluscs, but an exhausting human exercise in seeing how many of the little fellows you can extricate with a toothpick, dip lightly in the *rémoulade* or garlic mayonnaise, and pop into your capacious maw. It needs to be so, for those snails keep on coming. It's not supposed to be a race, but a steady eater near me must have done well over 100. I won't trouble you with my tally, lest you be still fiddling over your breakfast coddled egg, but suffice it to say, I kept my end up and the snails down.

There were about 300 eager eaters in the village hall, and about 20,000 snails met their end. We started with the melon and ham, then came the snails, followed by chicken roasted over a wood fire, cheese and salad, apple tart, coffee and Armagnac to steady the ship. The wine flowed freely throughout each course. It was pricey, mind. Twenty quid a head, but again, respectful of the *entente cordiale*, I didn't complain.

11 September 2011

NOT JUST THE ECONOMY, STUPID

So, just as the penny is beginning to drop about the economic pointlessness of overtaxing a tiny percentage of the population, up strides the boss of Marks and Sparks to proclaim his willingness to pay more income tax in order to alleviate the country's current economic woes. Not the first to say it of course, but he didn't get where he is today without spotting a favourable bandwagon. The idea was raised by the old Sage of Omaha himself, Warren Buffett, a man rich as Croesus, who has reached a stage in life where he realises that he can't take it with him, but has so much that he can't get rid of it fast enough. He wants to pay more tax to the United States and, as is always the case, wants everybody else to make the same noble gesture, to help the country get back on its feet again.

Now if I, a former mere bank clerk, know that this is a piece of window-dressing, you can bet Warren and the M&S bloke know it too. Whatever their generous contributions to their nations' exchequers, in the context of our economy, and the huge American one, the effect will be as a duck farting in thunder.

Pay more tax? Give it a rest. Not just punitive rates of income tax, we've got road tax, council tax, stamp duty, inheritance tax. Even the good old bank deposit account, where we put aside for a rainy day what's left after the first moiety of taxation, and then find ourselves taxed again on the interest. By all means, pay more tax if it makes you feel better, but spare us the grand gesture.

For those living in the real world there are more practical ways of helping than throwing your hard-earned money at the taxman, to be lost in the great bottomless pit of the economy. There are many thousands of sick, helpless, underprivileged, abused children in this country whose lives could be made a lot better with your help, and thank goodness that you do. Only this week I spoke at a dinner where, despite that disincentive, the BBC's Children in Need Appeal raised £2,500.

Earlier, I joined other charity workers at a major City trader, BGC, as they gave us all a day to pretend to trade. I traded a modest £30 million deal, but don't ask me how. The important thing, apparently, is to shout, 'Mine!'. Hopefully we'll net a six-figure sum when all the trades are added up.

There'll be shows, dinners and concerts as we run up to the big night, all raising big sums for Children in Need. But in the end it will be the unsung efforts of the cake-bakers, the fancy dress parties, the folk prepared to endure haircuts and immersion in baths of beans to make their small, but much greater, gesture that will make all the difference. It isn't all about the economy.

18 September 2011

THE FULL ENGLISH

It's been nearly fifty years since the first pizza parlour lured British diners with its tasty toppings, but a recent 'strategies survey' of more than 2,000 tomato-stained consumers has found that Italian cuisine has overtaken honest British fare as the nation's first choice when dining out.

Let us not waste valuable eating time questioning the validity of yet another example of pointless research, but who are these 2,000 people? Have you ever, or do you know of anyone who has been stopped in the street and asked whether they prefer macaroni to fish and chips? Me neither, but I know how these things are done. A busy shopper, suddenly accosted by a young person with clipboard:

'Hello. Can I stop you and ask you some questions?'

Shopper: 'What? I'm in a hurry, sorry.'

'Well, can I ask you if you prefer Italian food to British?'

Shopper, flustered but relieved not to be asked for money, rushes away to avoid further embarrassment: 'Yes, yes.'

Anyway, what happened to chicken tikka masala? It seems like only yesterday that the Indian dish was the popular choice. Don't try to tell me that Britain's diners are settling for a slab of stuff that's barely one up on a quiche to settle their stomachs after an evening's quaffing at the pub.

Even if we believe the survey, it's unfair. There are thousands of pizza joints and pasta places, but where do you go for 'British'? Pie and mash never really got beyond Hackney; bangers and mash are microwaved pub hell; and when did you last see a steak and kidney pudding on your favourite restaurant's menu? I know of one or two that throw in the odd bit of pork crackling or the occasional whelk as a gesture to our proud gastronomical tradition, but they're few and far between.

British beef is so far-famed that even the French, who think that they invented not only cuisine but food itself, genuflect in the general direction of the rosbif of Old England. But my personal survey shows a marked tendency in some of our ritzier places, to which the BBC invites me to trot out something with a Japanese name that has been massaged with beer since calfdom. The only surprise is that they don't ask us to eat it raw, like their fish. Oh, sorry, I was forgetting about 'tartare'.

Please don't confuse this with a xenophobic rant to draw our wagons in a circle and refuse all foreign muck, for it's been my limited experience that 'national' cuisines can be over-rated, particularly in their country of origin. The worst Chicken Kiev I've ever tasted was there, in the Ukrainian capital. Peking duck was truly revolting in Peking itself, and guess where I had my worst ever Irish stew?

2 October 2011

THE EMPEROR AND HIS CLOTHES

Art's a tricky old game. It used to be easy enough to tell an artist from an eejit by asking the simple question: 'Can you draw?' However, over the past hundred years or so it's all gone a bit blurry and the subject has become indefinable.

Apparently, nobody can say what 'Art' is any more without being lampooned on all sides as an ignoramus. If you can't make head or tail of Picasso, you're a Luddite. 'The eyes following you around the room' is no longer the sign of a good portrait painting, and if you think the whole point is that the work should look vaguely like its subject, you've lost the artistic plot. It's not about that tired old representational stuff any more; we artists are all free spirits these days! Who is to say that this old lavatory bowl, this pile of bricks, these cattle droppings, are not works of art, if I say they are? Define me 'Art' at your peril.

Last week brought us a splendid example of 'It's Art because I say so'. The Birth of Baby X will be the latest oeuvre by 'performance artist' Marni Kotak, following exhibitions in which she exposed intimate parts of her life to critical acclaim. This exhibit, at the Microscope Gallery in New York, will be her most profound and physically challenging performance to date. 'Giving birth,' says the bold Marni, 'is the greatest expression of life, the highest form of art.' Nobody cheering and applauding at this huge breakthrough will take Marni aside when the great moment is over and whisper: 'But, Marni, Art should be original. Even as we speak, the seven billionth human is similarly being brought into the world.'

I can already hear Marni and her friends' derisive laughter at that backward observation. Nor is that the end of the artistic performance: Miss Kotak's next magnum opus will be Raising Baby X, from the child's birth to attending college. I predict that this 'authentic personal experience' will run and run . . . that poor child.

Whatever happened to the old cry, 'The Emperor has got no clothes'? Even if it's as simple as 'I don't know anything about art, but I know what I like', nobody wants to be scoffed at behind their back as a dumb-bell. But let's come out from behind the arras and say it: some self-styled 'artists' have as much right to call themselves that as do unlicensed plumbers, electricians and cowboy builders, compared with the real thing.

The real 'performance artists' are actors, dancers, musicians, singers, comedians – all performers who bring something new and exciting, and sometimes even beautiful, every time they put themselves and their art out there for public approval.

Life itself can be a bit of a performance sometimes, but art it ain't.

16 October 2011

RACING CERTAINTIES

In times of doubt and schism such as these, television can be such a comfort. Nothing ever changes in *Midsomer Murders* – people continue to fall like the leaves in autumn – and, most reliable of all, over a cup of Earl Grey and a chocolate digestive, there's *Escape to the Country*. No matter how enthusiastic the couples seeking bucolic Nirvana may be – 'What a charming en suite!' 'Just what we were looking for!' – every regular viewer knows that the cheery presenter is never going to make a sale, for over the long years nobody has ever bought a property: 'John and Mary have returned to Bolton to think seriously about their next move.'

However, the recent discovery of a 'neutrino' (which you might be pardoned for thinking is one of those mysterious miracle ingredients that ladies dab lightly on their faces, because they're 'worth it') that travels faster than the speed of light, thereby casting a black hole over Einstein's Theory of Relativity, and our perception of the universe, has put the cat among the pigeons. Our received truths are evaporating in front of our very eyes. The Germans can't count any better than we can; rugby players are no better behaved in drink than footballers; cricketers may, allegedly, cheat; Vincent van Gogh didn't commit suicide, but was shot by a disturbed teenager; and Shakespeare didn't write Shakespeare.

This last canard has been a dead duck for years, but has been given new wings by a movie called *Anonymous*. This trumpets the cause of Edward de Vere, 17th Earl of Oxford, as the real author of *Hamlet* and *King Lear*. The film-makers are even producing a package of lessons for American high schools, further to promulgate their theory.

The director of *Anonymous*, Roland Emmerich (whose previous triumph was *Independence Day*, about alien invasion), says his film aims to set the historical record straight: 'I think it's not good to tell kids lies at school' is Roland's view. Giving him the benefit of a doubt that he doesn't deserve, he probably hasn't heard that the idea of the Earl of Oxford's authorship of Shakespeare was first put forward decades ago by a Gateshead schoolteacher, rejoicing in the name of J. Thomas Looney. No, really.

So much, then, for Christopher Marlowe, Sir Francis Bacon and Mary Herbert, Countess of Pembroke. Can we even be certain of Charles Dickens? How can a mere hack have known so much of the human condition? We must be constantly vigilant, upturning every literary stone, relentlessly pursuing the truth – particularly when there's not the slightest chance of ever discovering it.

23 October 2011

SIEGE MENTALITY

It may be the season of mellow fruitfulness and all that stuff, but for those of us in the autumn of our years, this is a weekend to batten down the hatches and repel all boarders. In case you were hoping that all the masks and pumpkins in the shops were publicity for a new teenage vampire movie, let me break it to you gently, before the first ring on your doorbell accompanied by the menacing childish cry of 'Trick or Treat!' tears you from the television: this weekend is Hallowe'en.

The pumpkins and the 'trick or treating' are an American import, and while we thank the Yanks for the turkey that they brought us for Christmas, we were all content enough with: 'A penny for the guy!' Although, of course, the implied threat is the same: hand over the money, sweeties, cakes or biscuits or your front door gets raw eggs or a new paint job.

Nothing, be it Bonfire Night, travellers, students in tents, disappearing pensions or the rest of the rubbish that the long-suffering, tax-paying majority has to put up with, gets up the nose more than somebody's little darlings looking for handouts on a dark night, when they should be tucked up in their little beds. It brings out the latent curmudgeon in all of us.

A radio listener suggested offering chocolate-covered Brussels sprouts or toffee onions to the little folk, and seeing how they liked that. Others threatened bear traps and tar-and-feather contraptions in the bushes. It's all hopeless; the deterrent ruses have all been tried before and found wanting. The old pretend-we're-not-at-home ploy is doomed to failure. Three-year-olds see through it, and there's nothing more embarrassing in front of the neighbours than a little fellow shouting through your letterbox: 'We know you're in there!'

One of my loyal listeners tried 'We don't believe in

Hallowe'en,' only for one of the children's parents to say, 'My mother remembers you coming to our house at Hallowe'en when you were a lad.' This same old geezer, knowing that children are allergic to everything these days, wanted to put a sign up saying, 'Caution! This house may contain nuts!', but he knew in his heart that it was a futile gesture. Have your money ready. This generation won't be placated with a toffee.

A couple of years ago, a neighbourhood group decided to give Guy Fawkes a break, and set fire instead to the effigy of someone who has done more damage than a failed gunpowder plot: a Health and Safety officer. They didn't throw in the Health and Safety rule book, fearing that the resulting conflagration would burn the area to the ground.

30 October 2011

WHIZZERS AND FIZZERS

Having soldiered through the nightmare of Hallowe'en and 'trick or treat', I hope I find you relatively unscathed by the vicissitudes and dangers of Bonfire Night. It is my forlorn hope that your nose hairs have not been set ablaze by some toddler's careless swishing of a sparkler, and that I don't find you suffering the effects of a barbecued sausage, burnt to a frazzle on the outside and entirely raw on the inside. Firework displays have been lighting up the skies and frightening the animals in my fairly rural neck of the woods for at least the past week, and while I tug the forelock to no man in my appreciation of the colour and spectacle, my first reaction is that I'm glad I'm not paying for it.

It may well be down to my Irish upbringing. Hardly surprisingly given the explosive nature of my country's history, ancient and modern, fireworks were banned in the Republic when I was a lad (indeed, they may well be to this day). Although in what was called 'Bandit Country', on the County Fermanagh border between Northern Ireland and the Republic, the little roads twist and turn, so, as I saw for myself, the firework-less Irish had only to walk around the corner to the emporium in the North, where the necessary minor explosives were freely available, and carry home all the squibs and rockets their hearts desired.

However, I don't want you running away with the mistaken idea that you're dealing with a numpty who doesn't know a whizzer from a fizzer, a Dancing Daredevil from a Bursting Bombshell. I've watched a display in Venice that would have gladdened even poor old Othello's broken heart, and in Valencia, where the annual three-day-and-night 'firework and fiesta' riot seems to set the whole world ablaze, and leaves everyone drained of emotion and deaf as a post for days afterwards.

It was with this excess in mind that for many years I staged a radio firework display every year on 5 November. I hope that the discerning listener will remember it fondly as a haven of peace, possibly the greatest display ever not seen – not a peep was to be heard.

From all over the world came tweets, blogs and mail wildly appreciative of the virtual colour and spectacle lighting up the listeners' imaginations, as I described passionately every sparkle, flash and tumbling cascade of colour going through my head – and nary an untoward crash nor unexpected explosion to frighten the animals or delicately nurtured kiddies. As usual there were begrudgers who complained about the lack of parking and toilet facilities, and burnt-out fireworks on the carpet around the radio, but I like to think that there are some who remember, with a sigh, the solace of fireworks on the wireless.

6 November 2011

FISHY BUSINESS

It seems like only yesterday, but given the inexorable passage of time it was probably years ago that 'Meals on Wheels' banned paper napkins on the grounds that elderly customers were treating them as food (thereby missing the point that it was possible the old folk were still hungry after their meal, or perhaps found it difficult to tell the difference between the napkin and the meat and two veg).

It behoves us all to keep a wary eye on what's dished up to us these days, particularly fish. I've always enjoyed it, despite an Irish Catholic upbringing that decreed, under pain of the fires of Hell, that we eat fish every Friday, like it or not. The upshot of this was to put everyone – even those who might have enjoyed it – off fish for the rest of the week, and possibly for ever.

I managed to retain a love of the *poisson*, through the endless Sundays of my boyhood. The Da would pop me up on the seat he had made on the crossbar of his bike and pedal through Limerick to a tributary of the Shannon. There he would park me on the riverbank, with a corned beef sandwich and a bottle of lemonade, while he cast for trout. I saw the mayfly live its frantic hour of life, the swallows swoop, the snipe dart, heard the invisible corncrake with its strange call.

I've still got a weakness for corned beef, but I haven't seen the mayfly this many a year, nor heard the corncrake; but then, I haven't sat on many riverbanks lately, with all the time in the world to watch my father attempting to tease a brown trout to the hook. He didn't really care whether he caught a fish or not, it was the tying of the fly and the art of the cast that mattered. Just as well, because my mother wouldn't have cooked a fish if you paid her. We had eggs every Friday.

When the Da went sea fishing off the Irish Sea coast he'd come back with mackerel and sea bass, which the Ma would pass on to the granny, who was ready and willing to lay about gills, fins and scales. I've never eaten fish like it since, although a lovely man from Grimsby keeps us unfortunate southerners supplied with the magnificent bounty of the sea. The Da would have been shocked to find eel, pollack and mullet, all of which he regularly threw back whence they came, on the menus of the ritziest restaurants, but then he fished before the 'sustainable' word became law.

He wouldn't believe that some unscrupulous chippies are serving Vietnamese 'panga', farmed on the faraway Mekong, and calling it cod. Nor that not one 'lemon sole' offered to the American public was found by investigators to be the real thing. But then Dover sole doesn't come from there, nor Dublin Bay prawns from Dublin.

It's a fishy business, Watson. I suspect that turbot may well be a flounder.

4 December 2011

ANYONE FOR TENNIS, COBBER?

For those of us who have forsaken the day job and find ourselves nodding off of an afternoon in front of *Countdown*, the Australian Open tennis has been a boon. Wimbledon, of course, remains supreme, cool, classy, with no unseemly chanting, rarely a Mexican wave and only the occasional wayward pigeon to cause self-conscious laughter. Even the applause is muted for all but Tim or Andy.

But of the other majors, Melbourne is the one that most frequently keeps the old geezer from slipping into the arms of Morpheus. The French is clogged with red dust, and a mere walk down the boulevard for those brought up on the clay, such as Nadal and his fellow Hispanics. The rallies drift endlessly, from one baseline to the other, and you know Rafa will go on winning it from his wheelchair.

The US Open brings out the worst in New Yorkers: cocky, partisan, their noisiness only drowned by the steady stream of jumbo jets roaring overhead. The crowd look as if they'd be better off down the road at Yankee Stadium, eating their hot dogs and watching the baseball. The Aussie Open leaves them all in the ha'penny place: where else do they play a major tennis championship in the early hours of the morning to avoid the sun? Where else is the shrieking of Azarenka and Sharapova matched by the seagulls overhead? Only in Oz do the ballboys and -girls have to wipe up dead bugs crushed by the expensively shod feet of uncaring tennis players. The crowd is always one-eyed, in the great Australian tradition, when there's a local boy or girl playing, but they're not too proud to adopt: they have named the Belgian player Kim Clijsters 'Aussie Kim' ever since she had an Australian boyfriend a few years ago.

The television coverage is masterly: not a shot missed, not a cry unheard, not a bead of perspiration unseen, the drama of it all unfolding before our very eyes. Unfortunately, what's going on in our ears is enough to drive anyone to drink, long before the sun has gone down over the yardarm. For the commentators never draw breath. Every shot, every rally is analysed; and if it were only the tennis, we might have a chance to enjoy the spectacle, but, in between the endless banal chat, we're treated to continuous assessments of the players' attitude, motivation and character.

The star commentator, a former champion, feels free to share with us his droning opinions on anything and everything, including his favourite films and music. It's now too late for Oz, but before the next major, can someone tell the numpties that the best commentators know that it's not about them. As Bill Clinton might have said, 'It's the tennis, stupid.'

29 January 2012

CITY OF LIGHT

In my more vulnerable moments, it weighs heavily on my mind that you may think you're dealing with some numpty or bumpkin here, whose view of life is as through the wrong end of a telescope, who knows nothing of the finer things, the broader view of what Marcus Aurelius called 'the great web'.

Well, let me tell you that I was in Paris last week, so there. A friend of mine was 'varnishing' his paintings, whatever that may mean. There was no smell of varnish in the room where he was exhibiting, and I know varnish when I smell it; both my Aunt Kitty and my great-aunt Maggie were French polishers to Dublin's toffs and gentry. Varnish and rashers frying were the dominant smells of my youth.

But I see that I've already allowed you to lead me down a narrow blind alley, deviating from the sunlit uplands, the wider boulevards of life and, more particularly, those of the City of Light, its shimmering river, its magnificent architecture, its sheer romance.

I took the train. The French police checked my passport at St Pancras station, which furrowed the brow a bit, but everything turned out all right when the British police gave me the once-over in the Gare du Nord as I left France. I'm sure that there's a perfectly good reason: ours but to do or die, you know.

The Eurostar was a delight: helpful platform staff, charming French service, under the Channel before we knew it, off the train and straight into the less than welcoming arms of the Parisian taxi driver. The personalities of these winsome fellows run the gamut from morose to psychotic, and a 15-minute run can cost you anything from a tenner to 20 quid. Use the Metro.

On Friday evening, eager to be overcharged at some famous brasserie (there's one where you can pay £68 for a roast chicken), we decided to avoid the expense of a taxi, and five crowded into a smallish town car, one of us in the boot. It seemed sensible at the time, but not when we were pulled over by a van full of gendarmes who, as luck would have it, passed us as we swung around the Place de la Concorde, and spotted our booted fellow passenger through the hatchback window. In a trice we were surrounded by half a dozen riot police armed to the teeth, convinced they'd caught a gang of people smugglers. It's a good job they closed the Bastille, because the French don't really see the funny side of things the way we do; but after some stern words they sent us on our way. Our friend in the boot had to walk. He was late for dinner, but we kept a cold chicken leg for him. At the price of the chicken it was a sacrifice, but what are friends for?

12 February 2012

PASTIES AND PITFALLS

At the risk of reopening old wounds, I cannot let the recent pasty debacle just lie there, gone but not forgotten. For I too, like Dave and George, have suffered at the hands of pasties and pies: every one I've ever eaten has given me chronic indigestion, including one that I didn't even get a chance to eat, a foot-long Cornish pasty that for some misguided reason was included in an outside radio broadcast that I was presenting.

You may doubt the efficacy of introducing a huge lump of pie, stuffed with meat and two veg at one end and something sweet and runny for afters at the other, on the radio. Even allowing for descriptive verbal flights of fancy, you may feel that, without the visual, something was missing. And it was, as the Cornish giant, which seemed to have a life of its own, slipped between my fingers and the microphone and covered the floor of our outside broadcast vehicle to a depth of two feet. It didn't end my broadcasting career, but let's just say the show was over for the day.

Always embossed on the fleshy tablets of my memory will be a certain pie that, in a moment of weakness, I attempted to eat in Blackpool, just before presenting the Miss United Kingdom beauty contest on BBC TV, in those far-off days before Germaine Greer and other female activists put the kibosh on such displays of feminine pulchritude. I bit into that pie with every expectation of, if not Wagyu or Angus fillet, at least something vaguely chewable in the way of meat. What I got was potato. Just potato. Apparently a staple in that neck of the woods, it took this southern softie by surprise, and not in a good way. I made a total and complete mess of the beauty pageant, getting my information on all the contestants mixed up and unable to tell Miss Bristol from Miss Oldham. Again, it wasn't the end of a once-promising career, but it wasn't my finest hour, and I blame the culture shock of that pie.

And by the way, it was cold, so don't come to me for back-taxes.

8 April 2012

HAUTE CUISINE

A pigeon sits placidly on her nest in the branches of the plane tree. Very occasionally, as any self-respecting father-to-be should do, her partner sits in, to give her a break from the monotony. The sun shines warmly, and the little creatures take advantage, knowing better than the humans that you can never rely on the weather in this hidden corner of France, just that bit too close to the Pyrenees and the Bay of Biscay for comfort. A couple of little lizards scurry across the gravel, lured by the unseasonal heat and a red squirrel nonchalantly strolls about the grass as if he owned the place, with a splendid disregard for the neighbour's cat and the enormous buzzard that hovers lazily above.

I've eaten squirrel pâté in a friend's restaurant in Mayfair – and very tasty it was too – but that's the unloved grey squirrel, an import for which we have little to thank the Americans.

Nobody with an ounce of decency in their soul could possibly consign the beautiful red squirrel to the pot, any more than I can conceive of eating that magnificent deer that leaps and bounds among the vines, across the road and into the trees. And yet, I confess to a taste for venison. As with much of the meat we consume, you don't want to meditate too long on where it comes from.

On the other hand, if you pursue that train of thought too closely, you would never even look at an egg. The French have never been as picky as us about what they put in their mouths. When it comes to 'haute cuisine', of course, it's a different story. They invented it, and when it comes to culinary creativity they continue to lead the world, no matter what you hear about magnificent bistros in Barcelona and Bray.

It's a different story at the other end of their gastronomic scale. These are folk who, having imported a giant river rat, the coypu, from South America to eat the smaller local vermin infesting the ditches, now cull the rodent by the simple expedient of eating it. They give it a fancy name on the menu – it's 'the hare of the pond' – but if you happen to wander in a south-westerly direction here, *prenez garde*.

Who else but the French would even think of eating the slithery snail? And they eat them by the ton, as the loyal reader will recognise from my ramblings of last year, at fêtes called *escargolades*. I'm not ashamed to say that I await with anticipation an invitation to my next snail-fest. That's if I have recovered in time from the punishing rigours of the annual local *grenouillade*, or frogs' legs feast.

This year I'm going to build up my resistance at a *sardineade*, a sardine-eating marathon. A little conventional perhaps, but if the French will risk it, I'm certainly not going to let our side down. *Bon appétit!*

15 April 2012

CATS AND DOGS

Last week a listener wrote to recount an evening in a south coast hotel, many years ago, when a fellow guest burst into the residents' lounge with a triumphant smile on his jolly, rubicund face and announced to the small gathering of medium sherries: 'I've just been made the Minister for Drought!'

My reporter says that he doesn't recall any outburst of cheering from the other residents. There may have been some light applause, but it was a quiet hotel. The excited man was, as those well stricken in years will remember, the late Denis Howell MP, a former union official, top football referee and Minister for Sport. Yes, multi-tasking, even in those far-off days. And to add to his burdensome portfolio, the then Prime Minister, Jim Callaghan, had just appointed Mr Howell 'Chief Rainmaker'. It had been a searingly hot summer in 1976, with nary a drop of rain. And global warming hadn't even been invented. There was nobody to blame so a futile political gesture had to be made to placate a disgruntled public complaining about the heat, dry riverbeds, empty aquifers and hosepipe bans. And the popular Howell was the man designated by Jim to bring calm.

Apart from looking cheerful but determined, it's never been clear what the Minister for Drought was supposed to do. There was never a suggestion that he might lead us all in a nationwide rain dance, with some aboriginal medicine men flown in to shake a few bones at the cloudless skies. There was good advice from that perennial rock of sense, John Humphrys, who bluntly told us on television that there was no need to flush the toilet every time we went for a pee. As you might expect, there was typically British cheerfulness in the face of adversity: 'Save Water! Bathe with a Friend!'

As it turned out, the appointment of a Minister for Drought

was possibly the most inspired shot in the dark of Callaghan's career. Within hours of the brave Denis taking on an impossible task, the heavens opened, and in a few short days we were all up to our ankles in water. And Howell was rechristened 'Minister for Floods'. The good man modestly never took all the credit for the change in the weather, but he was later, and properly, rewarded with a life peerage.

Are we to learn nothing from the lessons of history? No sooner were severe water restrictions imposed to combat the present drought, with the dreaded hosepipe bans, than the rain started to come down in bucketfuls. Of course, they tell us that it's the wrong kind of rain, it's being gobbled up by thirsty plants, it's forming puddles and not seeping through to the aquifers. So, why didn't we appoint a Rainmaker months ago? We'd all be sitting pretty on our life rafts by now.

29 Apr 2012

BLOOD AND SAND

The little town in south-west France has an open-air market every Friday. The main square and all the side streets bustle with stalls selling fresh fruit and vegetables, cheeses, sausages, hams and every possible permutation of duck. On one corner they're grilling chicken and quail, on another you can taste the local Armagnac before buying. And before you start accusing me of turning into a poor man's Elizabeth David, they're also selling those dreadful shirts and frocks that seem to be a French speciality.

For the rest of the week, it's the ordinary business of any French town, but this is a place that makes its prosperous way in the world by parties. Night markets feature every week in summer, the stalls selling not just cold dishes but cooking duck, guinea fowl, chicken and chips. There's much buying and selling, chatting and eating at trestle tables, while downing the local rough red.

On the bandstand in the main square a man plays an accordion. I always feel disappointed that it's all in colour. It should be in black and white, like those old French movies of my youth. It gets bigger for Tempo Latino, the place given over for a week to every ragamuffin and strolling player who wanders in with a couple of chords on his guitar. Tapas bars seem to spring from the very ground, and music is everywhere, with much tempestuous clicking of heels and castanets. Again, rather than have you accusing me of aping Hemingway, the odd reveller can be seen footless and the worse for the demon drink, but you can't make a Spanish omelette without breaking eggs.

Last weekend, Pentecost, as always, was a feria; for this town, like some in the south, has a bullring. Once more they flood in, berets, red scarves and all, from as far south as Barcelona, from the foothills of the Pyrenees, the Basques from the Atlantic coast, all eager for the ritual of blood and sand. I went once: it was more blood than sand. In Portugal, I saw a spectacle that was all sand and not a drop of blood. Out charged the bull, looking for trouble, only to be puzzled and teased by an elegant horseman carrying no cruel lance, just skilfully high-stepping away from every bullish rush. Then out strode the lads of the village, inviting the animal's charge as they darted in to snatch a ribbon from its horns. The ancient Minoan culture lives on: as a finale, they all attempted to spring over the bull's horns.

Surprisingly, nobody died, certainly not the bull. A herd of cows entered the arena and the bull, no fool he, joined the gang and they all trotted off like any well-behaved herd to the ringing of the lead cow's bell. You couldn't say that the bull won, but at the very least it was an honourable draw.

3 June 2012

GOLDEN MOMENTS

There's been a Brazilian rainforest-worth of description, opinion and comment on the great Jubilee, and while everybody, not least Her Majesty, would welcome a respite and a chance to lie down in a darkened room for a long period of rest and reflection, you sorely misjudge me if you think that I'm going to pass up on the opportunity to give you my thoughts, as an insider, on the Queen's Great Occasion.

Yes, I was lucky enough to be closer to the action than many, and the proud recipient, along with 12,000 ballot winners and charity guests, of a special Jubilee picnic hamper, which everybody tucked into with a will in the Palace garden before the great concert. And if you were wondering what Heston Blumenthal had done in the way of molecular gastronomy to merit that seat in the royal box for the concert, look no further than the aforementioned hamper. For the picnic menu was his creation. In the interests of more mundane tastes, old Hest reined in his natural instincts to try us with bacon and egg porridge, or foie gras done up to look like a mandarin orange.

A chilled British country garden soup would probably have worked better on a warmer June evening, but nobody gets hot stuff at a picnic – apart from my late father-in-law, who always insisted on bringing a Primus stove to the family's picnics in the Dublin Mountains, the better to enjoy his usual Sunday lunch of hot soup, boiled ham, potatoes and cabbage, prepared by his long-suffering wife while he took in the scenery with a nourishing bottle of stout. If you remember the erratic performance of the Primus, you'll understand why the family always returned home drained of all emotion.

'Best of British Potted Duo' sustained the loyal note for the picnic hamper mains, although English Breakfast might have been a more appropriate choice than Lapsang Souchong tea with which to smoke the Scottish salmon. The old favourite, Coronation Chicken, was replaced by a Diamond Jubilee bird that certainly tasted fresher, as well it might, after 60 years. The pudding was Sandringham strawberry crumble, and if your sweet tooth was still unsatisfied, Madeira cake, although again a Victoria sponge might have been a more suitable choice. There was West Country farmhouse cheddar, with biscuits that could only have been Duchy Originals. And it all came with a voucher that could be redeemed against a glass of champagne or beer.

It's a good job the picnic was over, and everybody around the front for the concert, when a rocket broke loose from its moorings during the magnificent firework display at the finish and zoomed over the Palace to crash into Her Majesty's garden. Thank heaven Madness had vacated the roof – and that Alan Titchmarsh wasn't there, pottering about the garden shed.

10 June 2012

ROYAL WARRANT

The disturbing news that rascally poachers are loading up buckets of our noble native snails and selling them to French restaurants put me in mind of another of our delicacies, which, if not endangered, and not being pinched, you don't see much of these days: the tinned sardine. Those of us long enough in the tooth to remember the hungry post-war years will recall the little fellows with mixed emotion, for they seemed to be everywhere: on toast, in sandwiches and in your salad, along with the half of boiled egg and a sliced tomato, with a dash of salad cream. And while you're there, where did that go? Anyone see a bottle of the gloopy stuff around lately?

The tinned sardine was a staple, liberally encased in olive oil, something barely heard of then, and of which we were more than a little suspicious, draining it from the tin before scooping out the silvery bounty. It is said that the late Lord Mountbatten, a deal more sophisticated than the rest of us at the time, would always bring aboard a supply of the finest tinned sardines when he joined a ship and insist that the tins be turned regularly, so that the fish benefited from an even soaking.

Oh, I know the gourmets among you are saying that sardines are freely available in the finest restaurants, chargrilled fellows, standing up on their own two fins, or griddled, hardly out of the sea, in some Portuguese fishing village. Sorry, they're not the same fish I remember. My sardines were tiny compared with these new, fat impostors. They didn't have heads either: no dead eyes staring up at you, and if there were bones, I never noticed. Head-less, boneless fish: a boon to mothers of small children everywhere. Although I suppose the ubiquitous fish finger covers that these days.

That's another thing, anyone seen a pilchard lately? A close relation to the sardine, but burlier, and similarly encased in a tin, this time in a rich tomato sauce. A shame that they also appear to have left us, for they were a source of consolation to many, particularly my friend, the lovely Rabbi Lionel Blue, familiar to you from 'Thought for the Day'. Every night, before he went to bed, he would make a pilchard in tomato sauce sandwich and place it just out of reach of the bed, so that if he woke up the next morning unwilling to face the challenges of the day, the pilchard sandwich would lure him from his trundle bed, get him on his feet and send him on his way, sustained.

This week I was among the lucky thousands to greet Her Majesty and the Duke of Edinburgh on their visit to Henley-on-Thames, and avail myself of a seat in her royal box at Wimbledon. A privilege and a particular treat, for teatime in the royal box is the only place in the world where they still serve sardine sandwiches. And not just without heads or bones. No crusts, either.

1 July 2012

A NIGHT AT THE OPERA

Last Sunday I introduced the first opera ever performed on a beach. Garsington Opera's marvellous production of Offenbach's *La Périchole* was beamed all the way from its magnificent location in the Getty family's estate at Wormsley to the sweeping sands of Skegness, queen of the Lincolnshire coast. It was all part of a splendidly ambitious project called SO, started a couple of years ago by the local council, not in any way to change 'Sunny Skeggy' from its well-loved bucket-and-spade, fish-and-chips image, which has served the town, and millions of happy holidaymakers, so well for many a year, but to expand Skegness's appeal, by way of art and culture.

So a great screen was set up on the very beach itself, and the opera performed, as seen by the black-tied audience in the award-winning glass and steel theatre at Wormsley, to thousands sitting on the sand, while donkeys took their children for rides and the adults vainly tried to keep the beach out of their sandwiches. An ambitious experiment that succeeded well enough to be tried again, although a greater attendance of the male section of Skeggy's population may be anticipated next year since the opera won't be competing with a Euro 2012 football final.

I've been an opera lover since my late teens, when my pal Ken and I offered our services as 'extras' to the Dublin Grand Opera Society's productions, as a way of getting in for nothing. I have trodden the boards in roles as disparate and demanding as a waiter in *La Traviata* (wearing suede shoes, an anachronism that infuriated the Italian producer) and a blacked-up slave in *Aida* (the things we suffer for our art, love). All 'popular' operas, as I'm not too good on the heavier stuff, never quite making the full circle of Wagner's *Ring*.

So, *La Périchole* was a new one on me, and I didn't expect such a riotous, jolly, laughter-filled musical comedy that was a lot closer to the Gilbert and Sullivan of my youth than we're supposed to expect from 'grand' opera. And there's the rub, as far as some of my fellow opera lovers are concerned. For them, opera is a serious business; a stiff, formal experience. They think it's wrong to laugh, in case their neighbour will think them unworthy of their seat at a cultural event.

They're even afraid to applaud, in case nobody else does. It's a self-conscious nightmare, and such a contrast to my experience of opera in Italy, birthplace of the musical form. In Verona, in the Roman amphitheatre, the crowd cheered and applauded every aria and chorus. It felt as if they were not far from singing along. They even insisted that the tenor sing an encore, something I've never experienced here.

Let's have more beach opera, then. Nobody's suggesting that you turn up at Covent Garden in sandals and shorts, but the stuffed shirt is a thing of the past.

8 July 2012

FIELD OF DREAMS

I'll admit it, I'm going to watch the Olympics from a distance. The news that only a minority of the thousands of spectators expected for the rowing events around Windsor are bothering to avail themselves of 'park and ride' confirmed my worst fears of the traffic gridlock that will inevitably bring the Thames Valley to a grinding halt, and make the usual standstill on the M25 look like a teddy bears' picnic.

As for travelling into London by car for the next two weeks, forget it. As it is, half the City will be 'working from home'. And before you ask, no, I didn't apply for tickets, another shrewd decision vindicated by news that the beach volleyball ladies may abandon bikinis in favour of singlets and shorts. Don't tell Prince Harry. I know that these sentiments may appear carping, and even provoke harsh words on a failure to join in the nation's upsurge of pride, and commitment to making London 2012 the greatest Games of the new millennium. 'Begrudger' and 'curmudgeon' are the mildest terms of abuse I have seen hurled at anybody who has been foolish enough to question the wisdom of the repressive powers granted to Locog by Parliament in the happy haze of the 2006 Parliament Act.

Before you start shouting me down, I'm a supporter. If we can ignore the posturings of the Mayor and every other politician from the Prime Minister down, seeking to bathe in the reflected glow of the Olympic flame, these Games should not only bring glory, but also encourage the nation to stop marking time and resume marching forward. I've seen what a successful Olympics can do. For several unforgettable years, when BBC Radio 2 was the corporation's radio sports channel, I presented the Commonwealth Games from Edmonton, Canada, and three Olympics: Montreal, Los Angeles and Barcelona. I'll pass lightly over

Montreal, where an ambitious mayor stretched the city's resources to a breaking point from which it took years to recover. I missed Athens, Radio 5 Live and younger, fresher voices having taken over the microphone. I did see the aftermath: disused stadiums choked by weeds, a lesson that I'm sure Lord Coe has taken on board. It was refreshing to read Peter Ueberroth, the mastermind of Los Angeles – the only Games until then to show a profit – saying that his inspiration was the 1948 London Olympics.

In 1984, Los Angeles, a city that had been ablaze with violent protest and racial disharmony, was transformed by its Games, seeming to bathe in a glow of peace and harmony. Barcelona in 1992 will never be forgotten by anybody who was there, for the sheer joy that enveloped the city and everybody in it.

Now it's London's turn to light up a war-torn, stumbling world. I'm sure that it won't be just distance that will lend enchantment to my view.

29 July 2012

LEGACY

So I return, fresh-faced from foreign parts, to heartening tales of the miracle that was London during the Olympic Games: courtesy, smiles and the kindly gesture from all sides. But, better than all the bonhomie, the traffic. Nothing, apparently. Where the cynic expected clogged motorways, jammed highways and immobile streets, all was sweetness, light and wide-open spaces. London and its attendant feeder lanes were empty and stress-free, with plenty of the 'After you, Claude', 'No, after you, Cecil', spirit that characterised the good old days—so winsomely portrayed in *Parade's End* and *Downton Abbey*, before the Kaiser caused the roof to fall in.

It was with light heart, then, that I took to the road in my old jalopy and headed for the Smoke on bank holiday Sunday. Twenty miles from town I joined a jam that did not unstick itself for the rest of the journey. On Tuesday, risking all, I made the same trip, and ground my molars to a fine dust as the motorway again came to a halt. Hours later, as I struggled home in the gathering gloom, I was caught in two more hold-ups. So much for 'legacy'.

I watched the Games, every magnificently televised minute of it, from afar and gloried in the nation's pride in a towering achievement, a timely restoration of the national spirit, hopefully a return to the old self-confidence and purpose of this country and its people. And without wishing to put a damper on those advocating a new national 'team spirit' after the success of Team GB, that success was founded on individual performances. It was the athletes, boxers, cyclists, gymnasts and most of the other medal winners who made Team GB shine so brightly. The team games, apart from rowing, boating and horsing, cast a dimmer light: ladies' and gents' football, beach volleyball, hockey, formation drowning, relays. Brave efforts, but no cigar.

Britain invented team games ('Play up! Play up! and play the game!') but it is in individual heroism that she stands alone: Gordon at Khartoum, Churchill in the Blitz, McDowell at the Ryder Cup.

At the risk of tedium, throw another log on the fire and I will relate a true tale that exemplifies that spirit of British grit, grace, nay glory, under pressure. It was a gloomy day at Lord's, 'neath rain and thunderous skies, and in the lull while players and gentlemen took early tea the late, great Peter West – who, had he been at the Olympics, would have commentated on everything from rowing to diving, badminton, dressage, judo and back – was filling the broadcasting void by standing outside on the roof interviewing the heroic former England captain Ted Dexter, who was holding an umbrella as the elements crashed above.

'Ted,' said Peter, 'what do you think of the game so far?'

'You'll have to excuse me for a moment, Peter,' came the reply, 'but I think I've just been struck by lightning.'

2 September 2012

MIRROR, MIRROR

Rabbie Burns thought it might be a help if 'we could see ourselves as others see us'. I'm not so sure. Does anybody really want to know what the world thinks of them, apart from the masochistic professions such as politicians and football managers? Self-knowledge is a laudable trait, but finding out what even your nearest and dearest truly think of you could mean half the population would never leave home and would spend their lives peeping out from behind the curtains of the front window, while the other half walked about with paper bags over their heads.

But never mind how others see us, we don't even see the real us when we look in the mirror. We can't, or we refuse to, see the view from our rear, of course, which has led to the perennial query of every female since we crawled from the primeval ooze: 'Does my bum look big in this?' To which the answer, from any male with half a brain, is always a resounding 'No!', whatever the truth of the matter. The real truth is that she can tell, even with a sideways view. The lady just doesn't choose to believe it.

How many times have all of us thought of a passing pedestrian: 'Who let him/her out, dressed like that?' Too-short skirts and even shorter shorts over little fat legs, making the wearer look like a 'barrel of bread-soda', as the granny used to put it so well. How often do we watch the television and cry out: 'Where did he get that tie? Why doesn't she brush her hair? Who told him to button all three buttons on that jacket? Why doesn't somebody tell her about her eye make-up?'

And it's no use blaming the make-up artist, it's their own fault. Like the rest of us, these people look at themselves carefully in the mirror and ignore what they see before them. It's not just the Wicked Queen in panto who shouts: 'Mirror, mirror on the wall, who is the fairest of them all?' Like that sad old boiler, our mirror lies, too, because we don't want the truth any more than she does. How else may we explain the bizarre appearances of film stars, celebrities and all those clinging to a disappearing youth whose ballooned lips permanently pout, whose immovable, seamless features look like something Lord Carnarvon dug up in the Pyramids?

Thanks to implants, facelifts and injections, with permanently frozen expressions the stars of yesteryear don't look like themselves any more, and nobody can tell them, because they look in the mirror and everything looks great: 'Begone lines, crow's feet and wrinkles, I look 20 years younger!' All is vanity.

We'd all be better off with the Edwardian common sense of my old granddad, as he dandled me on his knee: 'My face, I don't mind it, for I am behind it. It's the fellow in front gets the jar.'

30 September 2012

TIME, GENTLEMEN, PLEASE

It was the comeback of the century. Last Sunday's extraordinary victory by the European Ryder Cup team over their American rivals – and on the States' own turf, Medinah, Chicago – was a triumph to be long remembered wherever old golfers gather around the 19th watering hole. A triumph vitiated only by the chorus of disapproval rained on the curly head of Rory McIlroy, the young lamb having failed to adjust his timepiece between the Big Apple and the Windy City and turning up on the tee for his vital match with only minutes to spare. Fruitless to speculate how someone who has spent much of his young professional career on a plane, zipping across time zones from China to San Francisco and everywhere in between, could be in ignorance of the time of day, wherever his golfing talents took him.

What gives pause is that Rory was in Chicago for at least four days before giving a thought to where time's winged chariot had taken him. He must have been an hour late not only on the Sunday, but on the practice day, then Thursday, Friday and Saturday as well. And nobody, from his captain, José María Olazábal, on down to his caddie, said a blind word of caution, not to mention: 'And what time do you call this, then?' Young Rory should thank his lucky stars that he won his match against America's shining star, Keegan Bradley; if he'd lost, he might as well have shaved his curly head and spent the rest of his life in solitary contemplation in a cave in the Himalayas.

Someyears ago, Ireland's Luckiest Woman and I thought to savour the myriad delights of Las Vegas. As we crossed a time zone at the great Boulder Dam, I assiduously put my watch back by an hour to local time. Las Vegas was all we expected, and more: Paris and the Eiffel Tower, New York and the Statue of Liberty, the Pyramids and Sphinx of Egypt, the canals and gondoliers of Venice, with Rome in between. We rose in the morning, only slightly discomfited by the mirror in the ceiling above our bed, eager for the sights of Las Vegas. As we strolled, it all seemed a little anticlimactic; the place lacked sparkle. And so the long day wore on.

We went back to the hotel, then out to dinner. I had booked a recommended Chinese restaurant for eight o'clock, but when we arrived it was the same sight we'd experienced all day – waiters lounging about, nobody else to be seen. I gave my name to the maître d', who seemed a little surprised. Still, he smiled as he said, 'But, sir, your reservation is not until eight.'

'Yes,' I said, 'eight o'clock, and here we are.'

'But it's only six,' he said. Yes, I'd put my watch back instead of forward at Boulder Dam, and we'd spent the whole day in Las Vegas two hours too early for everything.

You're not alone, Rory.

7 October 2012

THE PUBLICITY TRAIL

The leaves fade and fall and, just as it is with the big guns of the television autumn schedules, so also goes the literary world. The behemoths of the bestseller lists, the Rowlings and the Rushdies, emerge from behind their writing desks to bedazzle the book-buying public with their latest blockbusters. Now's the time for awards, festivals, lunches and signings. The author, no matter how successful, must now traipse around the country, hawking his wares, if he wants to hold on to his elevated position, signing each book with a personal touch and a smile that risks lockjaw.

I can't speak for the award ceremonies, my poor efforts never having troubled the judges, but literary festivals and lunches are usually a pleasure. The audience at least starts on your side, or they wouldn't have bothered to spend their hard-earned on a mediocre lunch or a hard seat in a tent. The crowd is lively, out for fun and laughter, rather than erudition, and in my experience has yet to turn nasty enough to break up the furniture or hurl the cutlery. I've worked the halls of Cheltenham, Chichester, Blenheim and Fowey, ballrooms and restaurants, and exited pale but unscathed. You learn as you go along never to follow the likes of Gyles Brandreth or Pam Ayres, for the audience will surely be drained of all emotion before you even get to your feet.

However, it's the book signings that separate the wheat from the chaff: the author can find himself at the end of a deserted supermarket aisle, with only tired courgettes and wilting spinach for company, or in a dingy corner of the bookstore time forgot, just as they forgot to tell anybody that you were coming. Then again, you can find yourself sharing a home-made ice cream with the jolly crowd who patronise the bookshop-café in Kirkham. In Nottingham, I'm behind a desk piled high with copies of my latest tome. Behind me are posters of my book, my name and photos. In front are two large placards featuring, again, my name and likeness. As I sign one of the books for an eager buyer, I hear a passing customer enquire of an assistant: 'Who is that?' In Reading the crowd is big, and as I sign the last book and rise, pale but determined, to leave, a young man approaches with what looks like a religious postcard. I sign, he smiles, but looks a little disappointed as he leaves. I turn to the manager, and he explains: 'He thought you were Terry Waite.'

14 October 2012

ANIMAL MAGIC

I kept a small herd of Charolais cattle once. Don't ask me why, it was too long ago. I didn't keep them for milking, nor meat, and, frankly, they frightened me. I walked among them once, in a proprietorial manner, but, believe me, when you suddenly find yourself surrounded by a crowd of horned beasts, staring at you in a manner that can only be described as intimidating, you get out of there, and quickly. Cows aren't friendly; they have a tendency to give you the shoulder.

I'm not brave around horses, either. Big things, they come up to you out of curiosity and, if you're not carrying a bucket of hay, scornfully walk away with a dismissive swish of the tail. Don't run away with the idea that I dislike our furred and feathered friends; like any good father, I have fostered pets aplenty. We had a goldfish, won at a fair, that lived far beyond its natural fishy span and had to be buried with due ceremony in the garden. And a hamster that choked on its bedding, and failed to respond to resuscitation by hairdryer.

We owned a large dog, a Weimaraner, with taupe pelt, huge paws and teeth, and light grey eyes that frightened braver men than me – particularly a friend from Ireland who, having stayed the night, came downstairs in his pyjamas for his morning Earl Grey only to be met at the kitchen door by this huge dog that immediately stuck its nose into his groin. Ten minutes later I found my friend still at the kitchen door, frozen with fear, afraid even to scream for help lest the dog be startled and make off with his crown jewels. He might still be there if my wife hadn't come down and shooed the animal away. I certainly wasn't going to be the one to do it; the dog might have turned its attentions to my pyjama bottoms.

I fear that animals simply don't respond to me any more than inanimate objects do. Just as when something rolls off the table and makes itself inaccessible under the fridge, so it is with the animal kingdom and me. Even rodents show me no respect. Time without number, I have trapped a little rascal of a mouse humanely, carried it carefully into a field and released it gently into its native habitat. The mouse is back in the house before I am. I'm sure it's the same mouse every time, but maybe they all look the same to my prejudiced eye.

I envy a friend who keeps alpacas, although again I don't know why, and I'm not sure he does. They don't look as if they would make for good eating, although I'm told you can get a decent overcoat if you could ever get up the nerve to get their fur off. Have you seen the way they look at you? Haughty. It would be like undressing a dowager duchess.

28 October 2012

CHILDREN IN NEED

Despite the economic downturn, the past couple of years have been record-breakers in terms of the amounts contributed to the cause by the British public, in their truly remarkable generosity. The little bear with the bandage over his eye, Pudsey, seems to strike a responsive chord in the nation's heart, and it's the people who give up their time to stand in the November chill with collecting boxes on railway station platforms, outside schools, at shopping centres and in 100 high streets that make the difference, along with 1,000 cake stalls, school dressing-up days and, yes, even bathing in a bathful of beans, that elevate Pudsey to the little chap's status as the country's best-loved charitable icon.

Pudsey's Big Night started in the foyer of a Hammersmith hotel in 1980. I was there, with Esther Rantzen and Sue Lawley (they've always had a couple of able-bodied women to hold me up) and on that mould-breaking night the public contributed £1 million in five hours. Remarkable, considering the idea of a 'charity telethon' was new to British viewers, and that certain elements in Auntie Beeb's dustier corridors weren't exactly enthusiastic. I remember the producer of BBC One's most popular comedy at the time, *It Ain't Half Hot Mum*, refusing to allow us a strapline at the bottom of the screen with our phone number and address, fearing it might detract from the episode. It took a few years, but everybody's on board now, and since 1980 the appeal has raised in excess of £650 million. I'd like to think that you can top that up to around £700 million this year, but whatever you can give, every penny will go to help the children.

It's the films of sick or handicapped children, their bravery and that of their families, that tug at the heartstrings, but we shouldn't lose sight of the real poverty that exists in Britain. Children in Need provides thousands of cookers and beds to unfortunate families who have nothing to sleep or cook on. People talk of the 'undeserving poor', who won't work and who spend their state benefits on drink and drugs. Whatever you may think of feckless adults, no child 'deserves' to be poor. As poor and hungry as one particular little boy I've been told of by a child welfare official. The boy had a free lunch in school on Friday, and didn't eat again properly until his next school lunch on Monday. In this day and age in Britain, you may think such Dickensian poverty impossible in a welfare state, but it's true. I've no idea how many more hungry children there are like that little boy, but I know that there are 1,000 heart-breaking stories like his.

But I've already asked enough of your generosity.

18 November 2012

APOCALYPSE NOW

'The End of The World is Nigh!' A clarion call that has echoed through the centuries, ever since man staggered onto dry land, looked up to the heavens and wondered what was keeping it all up there, and if it was all going to fall on top of him when he least expected it. The threat of Armageddon has been used by beliefs and religions ever since, to keep us all on the straight and narrow. Through the ages, seers, prophets, witch doctors and conmen have led their followers to places of safety from the oncoming Doom, claiming that the heavenly voices in their heads have assured them that they alone will be spared.

A hundred or more years ago a preacher in the United States, inspired by visions and voices, gathered thousands of his faithful around him and prepared them for the arrival of the Four Horsemen of the Apocalypse, who would, of course, spare them, while the rest of us were put to the sword. It clearly didn't happen as predicted, but the preacher and his people took the optimistic view that God simply forgot, and they set up a new church to get ready for the next arrival of heavenly retribution. That church now counts its followers in millions.

In these more secular times, the fear of potential cataclysmic disaster seems no longer to be about God's vengeance, but has reverted to our earliest ancestors' fears of what's out there, in the great beyond of the stars. A couple of years ago hundreds were persuaded that a heavenly body, passing uncomfortably close to the earth, would carry them off to a safer haven somewhere in the Milky Way. Another no-show.

The latest manifestation of this inclination of the numpty to believe anything extraterrestrial, and the more far-fetched the better, is taking place as we speak in a small town in the south-west of France, with the slightly unfortunate name of Bugarach, which I have spoken to you about before. There, inspired by an ancient Mayan prophecy, thousands have gathered to avoid the end of the world, which will be on 21 December.

You may wonder how the Mayan priesthood could have predicted such an event so precisely, more than 500 years ago, and not managed to foresee the conquistadors coming to annihilate them, but thousands of believers are making Bugarach boom, with the locals charging up to €500 a night for a bed in a barn. These people, for reasons known only to the extinct Mayans and themselves, believe that under the mountain of Bugarach (which bears a passing resemblance to the one in *Close Encounters of the Third Kind*), lies a dormant spaceship which, as all hell breaks loose, and the rest of us once again will be expected to cash in our chips, will carry them off to a bright new world.

Don't say you haven't been warned. But I'd still buy the turkey and put up the tree if I were you.

16 December 2012

SPRUCED UP

The news that my friend, the excellent John Craven, has just torn a pine, or was it fir, sapling from the ground with a triumphant cry of 'Geronimo!' brought back memories: it must be well over 20 years ago that I decided to invest in forestry in the far north of Scotland, a wild and magnificent land where the sky seems to go on for ever. But hardly had the firs/pines gone into the ground before I was being criticised as a despoiler of the local ecosystem, overturning the timeless order of things by having trees planted on a bog and upsetting the habitat of a pair of nesting dunlin.

Fool that I was, thinking I was doing myself and the environment a bit of good, planting trees on a barren wasteland and encouraging wildlife, when all I was doing, according to the well-meaning protesters who stood outside my house with placards, was damage to the planet. My little saplings were already drawing down acid rain into the local rivers, apparently. The fact that the owner of the land, Lord Thurso, found no difference in the water, which he tested regularly, was immaterial. The damage was done, and to save further recrimination and public flogging my little trees and I were forced to part.

So you may imagine my feelings on reading that there is a proposal to clone Douglas firs in order to combat climate change. And it appears that the accursed eco-busting conifers actually absorb more of the dreaded carbon dioxide than other trees. So there I was, admittedly unknowingly, doing my bit to save the planet and getting a kicking from not only the thinking environmentalist but also the popular press for my pains.

There's more: after 60 years, some of the pines are due for harvesting, but people are protesting against such brutal felling of trees because they will be an irreparable loss to the landscape. You don't think they might be the same sort of people who protested about the planting of my trees all those years ago? And you don't think that there just might well be a similar change of mind in, say, another 20 years, about wind turbines?

Except, thank the Lord, for this wonderful, joyous festival of Christmas. For my family, and I hope for yours, that can never change. Some years ago, when my children were smaller, their mother and I suggested that instead of the boring old turkey we might enjoy a couple of plump, delicious ducks. The children, with one voice, threatened to leave home. Nothing must change. We had the turkey, and have been careful not to suggest any such radical upheaval since.

I still complain, in traditional curmudgeonly fashion, about overspending on too many presents, but that is also part of our family's tradition. And nobody takes the slightest notice anyway. May your days be merry and bright. And try not to feel guilty about your Christmas tree.

23 December 2012

WINTER OF OUR DISCONTENT

The world turns and, having no alternative, we face the bright New Year with the fortitude of all those who've never really grasped the seriousness of the situation.

When I say 'bright', you know I'm toying with your emotions, because there's no getting away from it, even for cock-eyed optimists like ourselves: January is as black as your hat. A well-meaning eejit of my acquaintance once said: 'January and the winter is my favourite time of the year, because I get to see more of my friends.' After I'd struck him severely in the mazzard, I had to concede grudgingly that we all do huddle together more for warmth in winter. Ignoring those of you who may be reading this on your iPad on a sun-kissed beach somewhere exotic (and good luck to you, we're not jealous. Just look out for those little redback spiders in the loo, and a box jellyfish can see you off quicker than a shark. Oh, and sorry that you can't get a proper cup of tea), most of us at this time of the year like to sit by a roaring fire and roast our chestnuts. Red wine, as long as you don't stick a clove in it, and a poker from the fire, tastes better in January, and if it comes to that, and it already has in my house, so do a glass of Armagnac and a cigar.

The Dark Side did for Darth Vader in the end, but some things are better in the dark, for those of us of a certain age. Friends have been kind enough to say that I look much better in the dark, or with the light behind me. You can't fall to pieces just because it's gone a bit gloomy. 'Bright' is not all that it's cracked up to be anyway. You can have too much of a good thing; have a look at all those summer photos, with everybody squinting into the sun. Think of the well-documented dangers of too much sunlight; the ageing, the wrinkling, the peeling, the freckles.

Think of the smooth, baby-faced complexions of those monks

and nuns of enclosed religious orders who never go outside their cloister. Never mind Botox, or those miraculous anti-wrinkle creams that were all over the magazines and TV ads throughout Christmas; give your face a rest.

Sit in the dark, it's easy at this time of the year. While you're there, why don't you count your January blessings? It's too dark, wet and cold to play golf; the relations can't get to you in this weather; it's much too mucky and dangerous to try to get to the supermarket; you've a reason not to go to that terrible New Year party; and the menfolk can't be bothered to pull on their galoshes to try to make it to the pub. You've a ready-made excuse to throw another log on the fire, sit back, put your feet up and pretend to be asleep. You never know, somebody might even offer to make you a nice cup of tea, with a slice of that Christmas cake. Unless the grandchildren have thrown it out because it's past its use-by date . . .

13 January 2013

SURVIVAL RATIONS

You may recall my tale a couple of weeks ago of a little boy who had nothing to eat from the Friday afternoon when he left school until the Monday when he returned there. I know that it was hard to believe, notwithstanding the current economic gloom, that such Dickensian deprivation should still exist here.

Unfortunately it's all too true, and has lately been borne out by the news that some schools are offering breakfast to children whose parents haven't the time, resources or inclination to feed them in the morning. Noticing that so many of their pupils are tired and listless through lack of nourishment, these schools have responded by providing food. It can only be hoped that this fine response spreads to all areas where there is need, while at the same time recognising that schools and teachers have their hands full with educating children, let alone taking responsibility for their welfare.

It all comes hot on the heels of a campaign to change the nation's eating habits to more healthy options and fight the dreaded 'obesity' which, you'll recall, a former health minister once denounced as 'more dangerous than global warming'. This a week after some other numpty had declared global warming a greater danger to the world than terrorism. Of course, it's a holy and a wholesome thought that we should all take the weight off ourselves, and by so doing, the NHS, by a healthier diet, but we've all been around this block a couple of times before. The clarion call to purge ourselves of impure fats, salt, sugar and filthy fast foods in favour of a better, healthier way seems to come up every six weeks. It can only be a short time ago that the blessed Jamie came up with 'pukka packed lunches' for schoolchildren to replace the rubbish that their thoughtless mothers were carelessly cramming into the kids' lunch boxes.

Jamie's, by contrast, had soup in a Thermos, half a papaya with a slice of lime, ciabatta with mozzarella or prosciutto, a salad with cherry tomatoes and mixed leaves and a dressing, wrapped in cling film, of lemon juice and olive oil. But you're ahead of me; he probably left you as early as the 'papaya with a slice of lime'. The idea that a harassed mother, who hasn't the time or inclination to make her child a bowl of cornflakes for breakfast, will trouble herself to make soup for a Thermos and a salad dressing of lemon juice and olive oil wrapped in cling film is beyond parody.

The luxury of discussing more economical cuts of meat with the supermarket butcher, and the leisure to select only the finest fruit and vegetables, is not one enjoyed by a mother with young children hanging on to her coat-tails while she worries about paying the loan company's interest this week. For many people it's not about whole, organic, healthy foods. Horse meat in the beefburgers? They were cheap. It's about survival.

20 January 2013

THE LITTLE THINGS

It's always the little things: wasn't it a mayor of New York who discovered that if justice came down like a ton of bricks on the petty criminal, information was discovered that enabled the law to nail the big boys?

My concern over the tiny things that drive you to drink, you might regard as more trivial: the person in front of you at the supermarket checkout who, having painstakingly spent 10 minutes unloading their trolley, suddenly comes to the realisation that the goods need to be paid for. An apologetic search in the pockets, first of coat, then inner clothing, produces no result, followed by frantic rummaging in handbag, then purse, before – hallelujah! – the cash or card is produced.

Or, if you haven't made any plans for the rest of the day, it could be the slow emergence of the chequebook, the laborious signing, and then the even slower decanting of the goods back into the trolley. The rest of the world, having ground to a halt, can move wearily on again. A similar time-worn and draining phenomenon can be freely observed at the passport desk at any airport. Having spent at least a couple of hours uncomfortably seated in a plane, and then walked for the obligatory 20 minutes along endless corridors, you join a queue that drags its slow length along for another mind-numbing period in which the world appears to have stood still, again. Finally you make it to the yellow line that, under pain of death, may not be crossed, and the person in front of you, who has also been standing in line for the duration, wakes up to find that they have to produce their passport.

What they were thinking of for all that time, or why they thought they were standing so long in line, must remain one of nature's little puzzles, but there they stand, bemused, and the frantic search begins: the apologetic patting of pockets to no avail, then an ever more panic-stricken search through travel bag or backpack before, with a huge sigh of relief, the missing passport is discovered. Another numpty re-enters the country.

The big things mostly never happen. The sky doesn't fall, doom rarely comes to pass, our worst fears disappear with time. And some big things add to the gaiety of nations: the London Olympics, the Shard. I was privileged to rise up Europe's tallest building last week, and look down on the rest of you.

The experience was enhanced greatly by the charm and courtesy of police, staff, volunteers, security. Something marvellous was started by the attitude of the volunteers at the London Olympics. Warm and welcoming. It's something worth holding onto.

10 February 2013

TALE OF A TELLER

It's always disappointing to feel that, with a few grey hairs, you find yourself forgotten, if not quite gone. No longer the invitation to join the glitterati on the red carpet and pay homage to winners of Baftas, Emmys, Globes, Oscars and Stephen Fry. The flashing light bulbs of the paparazzi blind others now, the few autograph-hunters ask gently for a signature for their grannies.

More disappointing, however, is the realisation that I am one of the few people left in the country not called to account by Andrew Tyrie and his committee on financial affairs. I've met Andy, and can claim a passing acquaintance with Lord Lawson of Blaby, but the call has not come – and I'm no longer holding my breath. It's not as if I know nothing of the whys and wherefores of banking.

Long before Moody's, triple-A ratings and the birth of George Osborne, I served my time behind the counter of the Royal Bank of Ireland, Cattle Market branch, Dublin. At the risk of brag-gadocio, there was none swifter to separate the half-crown from the florin, the soiled from the clean banknote. The soiled were well in the majority, and heavy with the scent of livestock, as indeed were the market jobbers who paid them in.

And in those days of not just pence, but halfpennies and fiddly farthings, I bowed to no one in my speed at totting up the cash book. Many's the time the kindly manager complimented me on my neat wrapping of a bundle of used lodgement dockets. I can't help but wonder if Messrs King, Goldman, Sachs, Diamond, Merrill, Lynch, or J.P. Morgan himself had such a rigorous apprenticeship. It might have served them well, and avoided the consequences for the rest of us of banks throwing cash around like sailors on shore leave.

In my day, grunted the crusty former bank clerk, getting even a couple of quid from the bank was like squeezing blood from a stone. Banking was simple: the bank kept your money safe, and if you wanted a loan, hard luck. You could try the insurance company down the road for a mortgage.

What am I saying? It's exactly the same now, if you're a small business. It was different in other ways, though: there was a person called a 'bank manager', whose bonuses – if he was getting them – weren't reflected in his old tweed suit. He actually met customers, and even knew some of them by their first names. Whether he knew the first names of his staff is unlikely – he never addressed us by anything other than our surnames. There was a pecking order: manager, accountant, cashier, teller, porter, me. At a drinks 'do' for the staff, I addressed the accountant as Mr. 'No need for that at a social occasion, lad,' he said, 'just for this evening call me JG.'

I left the security of a permanent, pensionable position, lured by showbiz's siren call, for the rackety life of a hobbledehoy. Sometimes, when passing a farm, I wonder if I did the right thing.

3 March 2013

THE ALIENS HAVE LANDED

With economic and political disaster promising doom daily; the loss of triple-A threatening to turn into triple dip; Beppe and Bunga Bunga turning Italian politics finally into the *commedia dell'arte*; and David Cameron turning into 'Push Me-Pull You' over bankers' bonuses, it still behoves us to keep a weather eye open on the dark side of the natural world – and not just because the ubiquitous Attenborough instructs us. He seems wrapped up in climate change and melting ice caps, not to mention Africa and the Galápagos, at the moment anyway, and seems to be displaying little regard for the aliens attacking us at every turn.

While we fret about Romanian and other immigrants poised and waiting to sweep from the shadow of the Urals and over the Channel, engulfing this green and pleasant land with their foreign ways, has anyone spared a thought for the country's waterways, and the parlous plight of our native crayfish? Is it possible that no one cares a jot about the damage done to the ecosystem by the supposedly decorative water fern, parrot's feather, Australian swamp stonecrop, New Zealand pygmy weed, water primrose and the dreaded floating pennywort that puts itself about at the rate of eight inches a day? All block out the light, deplete the oxygen and strangle the little fishes. The Government has banned their sale, and we must pray that it's not too late.

Too late to do something about the killer shrimp, I'm afraid. A recent arrival on these shores, this giant alien will eat anything, with scant regard for its expanding waistline, and not just our own native freshwater shrimp, but any fish or finger it can wrap its fearsome jaws around. It has munched its way here from the Danube delta and can be observed, as we speak, eating all before it on the Norfolk Broads. An even larger predator is the

American signal crayfish, now lording it in every river, lake and canal, where it has done for our little native crayfish in no time.

These savage interlopers are not alone in spreading death and destruction beneath those apparently placid waters. What of the Chinese mitten crab, the dreaded Turkish crayfish, you cry. It can only be a matter of time before these alien monsters seek greener pastures, wider waterways to conquer. Then what will be the fate of the Dublin Bay prawn, the Cornish lobster, the common crab, the simple sardine?

On top of all this news comes that residues of sleeping pills and tranquillisers are altering the behaviour of our already belea-guered freshwater fish. In view of the dangers that lurk for them at every turn in the river, can we deny them their escape from reality?

10 March 2013

HIGHWAYS AND BYWAYS

Just when the long-suffering motorist in my little corner of this sceptred isle thought that the lanes and minor roads of South Bucks couldn't get any worse, along came the always unexpected winter snow, and now the even more unexpected spring variety, and 'Stone me!', as Tony Hancock used to say, they got worse. Potholes have turned overnight into archaeological digs, uneven surfaces to trenches.

Naturally, whoever is responsible has moved like a wounded snake, while a leisurely search is made to find a numpty to whom the buck can be passed. All is not lost, however. Someone has been found to take the rap. Well, when I say 'someone', it would be more accurate to say 'something'. For there, on a grievously afflicted little thoroughfare, stood a sign: 'Failed Road Surface'.

You see, after all, it's not the fault of the road-builders, maintenance workers and certainly not the district or county councils. It's the road itself that has let us down, failed us in our hour of need. This little road that promised so much has disappointed us yet again, caring not a jot for our suspensions, undercarriages, exhaust pipes, paintwork or tyres. Bad, bad road! No wonder nobody wants to do anything for you.

Some years ago, in the county of Cavan in Ireland, I met a man who set himself the task of drawing attention to the parlous state of the roads. He gathered up all the broken bits of cars, lorries and tractors strewn in the ditches, and took them to the council offices to show them the extent of their careless husbandry. He did more: at dead of night he toured the county, painting large yellow circles around the huge holes in the roads. The council prosecuted him for causing a nuisance and defacing the road surfaces. The concerned citizen, once again, got it in the neck. 'My life,' he cried, 'has become a living dread!' Despite the unsparing efforts of Superman, Batman and Spider-Man, nobody in authority likes a vigilante, or complainers from local pressure groups. They'd rather you paid your taxes and allowed them to have their tea and biscuits in peace.

The BBC, the Catholic Church, the politicians, the inept police and local councils . . . the list of the guilty lengthens and, just like waiting for a bus, we've been hanging around for ages in ignorance, with nothing but Leveson, the EU and the crumbling world order to divert us, and then, like buses, the tsunami of sex scandal and exploitation surges over the hill, all together, engulfing all in its path. And again, nobody in authority takes the blame. 'Not our fault', 'It wasn't me', 'Nobody told me', 'I'd no idea it was going on'. Close ranks, no need for sackings or resignations, keep your head down and look busy and it will all be forgotten. More tea? One or two sugars?

17 March 2013

THRIFT

The Prince of Wales makes his appearance on television, looking like Worzel Gummidge in a torn old jacket covered in patches. Branson's son and heir gets married in exotic splendour, but at the expense of *Hello!* magazine. The Duchess of Cambridge carefully recycles her outfits. As my great-aunt Mag used to say: 'It's not by throwing it around that they have it.' Thrift has replaced baking, with the right people, as the new rock'n'roll. Yet poor old George Osborne continues to get it in the neck for advocating good husbandry. The clarion call for general belt-tightening has failed miserably to strike a responsive chord with the public; Thatcher's children don't want to know. Old spending habits die hard. Just try to book a table at short notice at any expensive restaurant. If you're lucky enough to get a cancellation, have a look around when you get there, and see if you can spot an empty chair. They can't all be Russian oligarchs, Middle Eastern potentates, hedge funders, footballers or relations of Bernie Ecclestone. The great British public are in there as well, eating, drinking and carousing, with scant regard for where the next meal is coming from, not to mind a triple dip in the economy.

Yet we are told that there's so little money about that the Bank of England is going to have to print some more. I don't know if you've noticed, Mervyn, but people are still spending as if their pockets think their hands have gone mad. At the Cheltenham races record-breaking crowds threw money at the bookies, including my own countrymen, the Irish, in their thousands, despite their record unemployment, emigration and a banking system even more banjaxed than Britain's. It's all reminiscent of the last days of the Roman empire, before the Visigoths came swarming over the Seven Hills and down the Appian Way.

Some people are pretending that the worst is never going

238

to happen, raging against the dying of the pound. Not Prince Charles. His thrift, and that of his mother, is inbred. His thread-bare jacket is no affectation. The upper classes have always been careful with their money, if not parsimonious.

Over the centuries, the great and the good have learnt not to flaunt it; you never know which Viking, Saxon, Norman or tax collector is coming over the hill. Not for them the yacht, the private island, nor complaints to *Fortune 100* that their wealth was underestimated. The Duke of Devonshire wore the same old brown hat for years, and was born in his boots. Dress down, block out the windows, plead poverty. You don't want loose talk in the servants' hall. 'No kedgeree for me, Carruthers, this morning, just a frugal boiled egg. And supper on a tray this evening, we've had to let cook go. I'll be in the Van Dyck room, dusting the Michelangelo. Castle Howard have sold that Reynolds for nine million quid, tax-free.'

24 March 2013

YOU KNOW WHAT?

I know that we have enough to worry us, with the weather and the lights going out, and sundry loonies in charge of nuclear weapons, but can anyone save us from 'You know what?'. The verbal crutch has spread across television like a plague, sweeping aside even the ubiquitous 'Y'know' that has propped up every footballer's every second word since first spoken, continually, by David Beckham.

'You know what?' is far more insidious than a footballer's verbal prop, however. You can hear it virtually every time you turn on the television, from game-show hosts to golf commentators. And do you know what? This interrogative is never, ever followed by any information whatever, but invariably by something we already know: 'Y'know what? That was terrific.' 'Y'know what? That was a fantastic shot.' 'Y'know what? You're absolutely right.'

Nobody knows better than I do how easy it is to gabble on television and radio, to lean on a familiar phrase when searching desperately for the *mot juste*. In the early days of Irish television, which coincided with my early days in the medium, many a time I had recourse to anything my brain could dredge up, in those terrifying moments that anybody who has ever stood in front of an unforgiving camera will recognise, when a great silence descends and every second seems a lifetime.

Although, a couple of years ago, while presenting Children in Need, it was half a ton of steel that descended from the rafters above, to land with a resounding crash on the stage, a scant few feet away from me. A tad to the right, and the great silence would have been all mine. But since I was unaware of my narrow escape I had gabbled cheerily on, while all around me were reaching for the sal volatile. I don't know about standing inadvertently on an angry rattlesnake or stumbling across a sleeping tiger. My only experience of real, cold-sweating, mouth-drying terror – unless you count trying to address a drunken corporate crowd in the ballroom of the Grosvenor House Hotel – has been when the wheels come off on 'live' television.

Everything was black and white on television in those early days, so Irish viewers will hardly have noticed the suddenly pale face of a young presenter as, out of the corner of his eye, he saw the female singer he had just introduced crash to the ground from her flimsy stool, guitar and all. They will probably have detected his terror as he gibbered utter rubbish into the camera for the two minutes it took to rebuild the stool and restore the lady to her perch. The memory of those endless two minutes I will carry to the grave.

Another afternoon, I watched in horror as a commentator at a televised race meeting suddenly stopped in excited mid-flow and clutched his chest, speechless and stricken. It was riveting, not only for the horrified viewer but obviously the director as well, for he allowed the camera to stay on the unfortunate commentator, for probably only a few seconds, then at last, mercifully, the camera swung away. We heard later that we hadn't been watching a heart attack. In his excited chattering the commentator's false teeth had flown unbidden from his mouth and he had caught them on his chest. Unwilling to show his naked gums to the viewing public, he remained speechless for what to him must have seemed a lifetime before he saw the camera move away and he could restore his false teeth to their customary position. And people ask if I get nervous on television. My nerve ends were burnt away many years ago.

31 March 2013

A DOG'S LIFE

The other week I found myself sharing a sofa with a dog on live television, in a discussion of the week's affairs. Luckily it was in the dead of night, and not too many scathing comments have been passed, in my hearing, on the superiority of the animal's contribution compared with mine. The dog was asleep, as were most right-thinking members of the viewing public.

It was Andrew Neil's programme, and his dog. I don't know how often he brings it along to keep other television presenters off his sofa, but it's further confirmation of the anthropomorphism that epitomises the British attitude to animals: a dog wins a nationwide talent contest, rising above the paltry efforts of mere humans; another achieves fame by growling on television and is fondly imagined to be speaking, even if it can only say 'sausages'; a faithful mutt discovers its owner's long-lost ring, and no day goes by without an animal story, whether it's a housewife who was once brought up by monkeys, the non-performing pandas, or horses being treated better than children.

The dog as man's best friend was fully endorsed by the report of a driver, pulled over by the police for driving eccentrically, who claimed that it wasn't his fault. It was his dog that had been driving. The man's counsel, aptly named Foggo, said in his defence: 'My client is bored.' The state of mind of the dog didn't come up. It recalled a true story of another peculiar driving contretemps, in Ireland, where devotion to animals – apart from horses – is not so marked as here (although in a little town in the county of Clare I have seen a calf seated snugly in the back of a small family saloon).

An alert police patrol on an Irish back road spotted a car being driven in an unconventional manner, and pulled it over for inspection. No whiff of alcohol was detected, and the driver, sober as a judge, was surprised and not a little offended to be apprehended in such a manner. As he indignantly stepped from his vehicle, however, the reason for the car's uneven progress became apparent: in place of the two front seats stood two kitchen chairs. The driver was further taken aback by what he took to be the overreaction of the police to this discovery. It seemed to him that they were excessively concerned at the idea of a car being driven over winding country roads while the two front seats slid all over the floor. Was it not perfectly understandable to remove two comfortable, upholstered car seats and place them around his kitchen hearth, where he sat after a hard day's work, while replacing them in the car with his serviceable, but hard, old kitchen chairs?

It's to be hoped that the law didn't come down too hard on the fellow. The logic can't be denied: a car is for work, a kitchen for sitting.

April 2013

RED-LETTER DAYS

Forty-eight years ago, almost to this very day, the 'Luckiest Woman in Ireland', as I like to think of her, became my wife. The great occasion was filmed by the Irish Television Service on what was obviously a slow news day. It's gathering dust in an archive, just like my head, on a shelf in the basement of Madame Tussauds, and the black and white film only makes its appearance when someone wants to show how life was in ancient times.

The present Lady Wogan and I were known to the Irish public, me for regularly making an eejit of myself on Ireland's newish television service, she for her beauty, so a large crowd had turned out at the church in Dublin to make sure that I got my just deserts. To no one's surprise, the heavens opened and the crowd, getting out of the rain, followed the bride into the church. They swarmed into the pews and crowded up the aisles, joining merrily into the spirit of the occasion, applauding the responses, and shouting colourful advice on how to survive married life, as the happy couple made their way down the aisle.

We somehow weathered the storm of confetti, rice, rain and cameras and made our way to the reception, lavishly laid on by her father in a country club on the shores of Dublin Bay. And when I tell you that there was the unprecedented phenomenon of a 'free bar', you'll know that I do not use the word 'lavish' idly. By the time we sat down for the traditional three courses and wedding cake, the atmosphere in the dining room was veering on the vivacious. Vivacity progressed easily on to verbosity, hilarity and a tendency on my wife's father's part to burst into maudlin song. Only my mother's fierce grip on his coat-tails prevented my own father from launching into 'Dead for Bread' or some other Edwardian tear-jerker.

At a real Irish wedding, there is no protocol about the

speeches; after the best man, groom and father of the bride have had their say, it's every man, woman and child for themselves. Anyway, the father-in-law made the most of his hour upon the stage, and rose to his feet at every momentary pause in everybody else's speech, including my own father's.

A relative sent my wife the old invoice for the great day, which her father had long kept as a memento of his finest hour. The wedding feast for 126 people was 27s 6d (£1.35) a head, and the 'free bar', everything from Guinness to champagne, and open all day, came to the princely total of £180, in the old money.

21 April 2013

THE IRON LADY DEPARTS

Now that the captains and the kings have departed, and the last post sounded to the passing of a Prime Minister who, more than any other in our time, changed this country's path, and before time clouds the mind's already fleeting images, for my own sake, as much as anything, let me share my impressions of a noble, sad day. It was cold, with a sky that threatened rain, as we left the car near the Viaduct Tavern and made our way down Newgate Street and, although it was only 8.30 in the morning, through the crowds that had been lining the pavements around St Paul's since dawn to pay their tribute to Baroness Thatcher's memory. It was a long walk; we should have taken the Tube, as did Lady Susan Hussey, widow of 'Dukie' of fond BBC memory, and boon companion of the Queen this many a year. With her, a former great Speaker of the House of Commons, Betty Boothroyd, and undaunted, back they would travel the same way, fortified by a warming tincture at the Guildhall reception, held after the funeral. The nearest thing, I suppose, that the English get to a wake.

I was there early, giving my sixpence-worth of contribution on radio and television, and the first question I was asked was whether I was 'looking forward to the wedding'. Recovering, I recalled memories of a lady I could hardly claim to know well, but whom I'd interviewed on television, who had invited me to 10 Downing Street, but, best of all, given vigorous support to the Children in Need appeal by joining me on the night in the studio, something no Prime Minister since has found time to do.

It was not only the crowds and the media who had been there since the early hours; a queue of invitees was already forming outside the cathedral's locked doors two and a half hours before the ceremony was due to start – obviously aware that, unless you were high up in the lists of potentates, political leaders, family and the Queen and Prince Philip, it was divil take the hindmost as far as the seating was concerned.

Having given my all to Breakfast, Naughtie, 5 Live and Dimbleby, Helen and I joined the congregation at just before 10 and were shown to seats, well back in the nave, appropriate to our standing, along with various hobbledehoys, journalists and others equally surprised to have been invited. I had time to observe others of the lower orders ignore the gentle prompting of the ushers and make their way boldly to the front pews. We missed nothing, seated at the back; large television screens enabled us to see the whole of the sombre, magnificent procession of the gun carriage through the streets, before the arrival at the cathedral.

A day that I was privileged to attend, to live in the memory, and only slightly marred by that little waif who writes on fashion in the *Telegraph*'s sister newspaper, who claimed that she could see my nose hairs on the television.

28 April 2013

A BEAKER FULL OF
THE WARM SOUTH

While we pull ourselves together from the coldest winter and spring that most of us can remember, and reluctantly discard our thermogenic vests on the doubtful promise of warmer days ahead, the eternal optimists who advocate climate change, née global warming, have the brass neck to tell us boldly that with the ever-increasing warmth that we'll be enjoying in the years to come, Britain will be challenging Bordeaux, Burgundy and the Rhône as a producer of great red wines. Meanwhile, if all goes to plan, and the burning sun continues to beat relentlessly down, the once-productive vines of Bordeaux, Burgundy and the rest of France will shrivel and perish in the heat.

I hate to put a damper on this fine talk, but from my immediate vantage point in one of the lesser wine regions of France, there seems little evidence of blind panic among the growers as their carefully tended vines continue to march triumphantly in dead-straight lines over field and hill. They're cautious men and women, but they think that this year's vintage might be OK, if things warm up a bit. They continue the traditions of their forefathers, tilling the land, planting the crops, always at the behest of the seasons and the weather. They live longer around here than anywhere else in Europe, and it's not due to their diet, which admittedly has plenty of vegetables but also liberal amounts of spirits, wine and duck fat; there are no traffic jams, everybody has time for a chat and takes an hour and a half for lunch. Their only stresses are the changing seasons and the state of their crops.

This area has seen a century of war between French and English kings and a more recent occupation by Germans, and the locals seem unfazed by the shenanigans of the Elysée Palace, the failure of Sarkozy and, even worse, of Hollande. And there certainly would be little point in warning them that in some unforeseeable future, their hard work, and that of the generations before them, would be burnt to a crisp, and nothing left of their rich fields of corn, sunflowers and vines but desert . . . they would just look at the sky and think about what tomorrow holds.

The rest of us can hum this old tune by now. A good 40 years ago, a sage of the great warming warned that, by now, the streets of London would be deserted, swept by fierce, hot winds. Some 10 years ago a government minister advised that Britain's gardeners would be better off forgetting about planting their roses and other traditional flowers in favour of succulents, such as cacti, which would be better able to cope with the increasingly hot weather that lay ahead. He would have felt himself vindicated by the winter before last, when the reservoirs dried up.

Then, contrary as ever, last winter the heavens opened and it never stopped. The world turns . . .

5 May 2013

EYES ON THE PRIZE

These days, we're freely advised that the only route to survival, not to mind success, is to press on, eyes fixed firmly on the distant horizon. Look ahead; never mind what's behind you. Life's serious, not a pantomime. And yet, if you don't remember where you've been, how can you be sure where you're going?

I only mention it because I recently came across a couple of thoughtful critiques of my early television work, done just after the Relief of Mafeking, on a live lunchtime show titled, shrewdly enough, *Lunchtime with Wogan*. It was ahead of its time, as was made manifestly clear by its paucity of viewers, and it would be at least 15 years before the British viewing public overcame their sense of guilt about watching television during the day. None the less, the critics could spot an easy target when they saw one: a lady in the *Daily Mirror*: 'Wogan cods you along with that warm hot-water bottle voice and glides through the audience with the smooth control of one who might have spent a lifetime as a male nurse.'

One of the greatest of all television critics, the *Guardian*'s Nancy Banks-Smith, whose wit has never since been matched: 'The built-in hazard of such a show is not that someone in the audience may drop off, but that they may drop dead. Wogan has an Old English sheepdog, a discriminating animal that keeps trying to leave the stage.' I had completely forgotten that dog – I suppose somebody must have thought it was a good idea, to take people's attention away from the numpty presenting the show. Do you think that's why Andrew Neil brings his dog onto his late-night show? Only Attenborough can get away with sharing the stage with stars of the animal kingdom, although even he struggles with meerkats.

Children's television consists of mainly young adults behaving childishly; real children would steal the thunder. Like any small animal, children lack affectation and self-consciousness. Their unadorned spontaneity is what grown-up television presenters have lost, and spend their careers trying to recapture.

The old pros feared the child star, none more so than the great comic actor W.C. Fields. Appearing in a movie with an adorable curly-haired little cherub named Baby LeRoy, Fields spiked the innocent child's milk with a tincture of his own firewater just before a scene. As Baby LeRoy, under the influence, stumbled, Fields stopped the shoot. 'Hold it!' he commanded. 'Walk him around, the kid's no pro!' Of course, he could have been kidding.

Of a thousand examples of my own deflation at the hands of toddlers, I offer this: at an open day for a children's playground that I support, a little chap is sent running up to me by his parent, autograph book in hand. Shoving it under my nose, he cries, 'I don't know who you are!' It's the kind of thing that keeps you in check, like reading old crits.

19 May 2013

TWEETING

Sir David Attenborough's tweets for the songbird-starved are a welcome change of note from the incessant verbals of BBC Radio 4, even if the willow warbler gets better listening figures than Humphrys and Naughtie. It's always a salutary lesson for the preening broadcaster when the unregarded slips unnoticed into the schedules and lets you have it in the back of the neck.

I have personal experience of a couple of minutes of technical silence on the airwaves getting more listeners than my ramblings. A few years ago, the tightly wound rubber band that kept BBC Radio 2 on the air snapped, and me with it. The music, on a different rubber band, continued on its merry way. It was a scant five minutes before I was restored, but in the interim, schism and doubt had spread like wildfire among the loyal listeners. Knowing that nothing short of an asteroid ending all life on earth would shut me up, and having noticed no global disaster of such a magnitude, they reasoned that there was only one explanation: the Grim Reaper.

I've never had a greater reaction to a broadcast. For days afterwards, strangers would stop me in the street to tell me that they thought that I had gone to my eternal reward. They looked at me oddly, as you would a vampire, or one of the undead. I thought I detected a certain disappointment that I'd turned up, like when a really boring guest takes their leave of a party, and then, just when everybody is breathing a sigh of relief, walks back in again.

But I see that I've wandered off the beaten track . . . I'm a bird lover, but I've never tweeted in my life, and in the sylvan surroundings of where I'm lucky enough to live am daily woken by the racket kicked up at all hours of the morning by our feathered friends. The sweet song of the blackbird, the chirruping and warbling of indeterminate others are a joy, but I can do without the cawing of the crow, and the witless cooing of the pigeon.

Stop me if I've mentioned this before, but isn't it strange that the most beautiful birds make the ugliest sound? I know that it can often be the same with our own species, but the screech of the beautiful peacock, the bark of the jay and the magpie that belie their lovely plumage, and the scream of the recent interloper, the parakeet, remain a strange contradiction.

I've never kept a bird, even in a gilded cage, but we do have a cuckoo clock. It was presented to me by the European Broadcasting Union in Switzerland, following the speech I made at their convention in which I tried to explain why we find it hard to take the Eurovision Song Contest as seriously as the rest of Europe. I put it down to our sense of humour. Maybe their presentation of the cuckoo clock to me was a sign of theirs.

26 May 2013

COUNTING OUR BLESSINGS

A week or so ago, as I sat in France watching the rain lash relentlessly down, and the euros rising as steam from the swimming pool, I think I could be forgiven for questioning the efficacy of holidays. How exactly was sitting looking out at the inclement elements, which I could just as easily have been doing at far less expense at home, be doing me the slightest bit of good? I know that I'm leaning against an open door here with everybody who has sat glumly on holiday, looking out at the driving rain from tent, caravan, bed and breakfast or hotel, even one with carpets in all main rooms, and free use of cruet . . .

I hate to sound like Rebecca of Sunnybrook Farm, but we must count our blessings. It's not so long ago that there were no holidays, even rain-soaked ones. Apart from the tavern and music hall, the working man's rest and recreation were non-existent. Only Sundays were free of the coalface, mill, factory and field. It was a tedium changed only if you were hit on the back of the neck by a press gang, and suddenly it's a life on the ocean wave, dodging cannon balls, picking the weevils from the ship's biscuits, and scurvy. You could always take the king's shilling, of course, and try to stay alive under musket fire, bayonet charges and the sabres of the French cavalry.

Even if there had been holidays, there was nowhere to go. Most people lived and died within a couple of hundred yards of their mother. Unless you were Jane Austen, and the horse and cart took you to Bath, where you walked about in uncomfortable clothes, watched the elderly and infirm retching as they tried to drink the sulphuric waters and took a calming cup of tea before retiring to bed, wondering if all the excitement was good for you.

Blackpool, Bridlington and Yarmouth were for fishermen only, Greece and Italy belonged to history and myth, and as for sun-kissed costas . . . Nobody went to France, apart from the Scarlet Pimpernel, and a trip to the Med was only on the cards if you were kidnapped by Barbary pirates and sold into a sultan's harem. And only the reckless went to Florida, unless they wanted their scalp hanging from a Seminole tepee.

There were diversions: bare-knuckle fisticuffs that lasted 35 rounds, bear-baiting, cockfighting and public executions that lifted the jaded spirit and provided a light in the gloom and tedium of relentless work. Tyburn Hill was where Londoners went for a jolly holiday, eating and drinking as they watched unfortunates swing from the gibbet.

Every year, as I present the live musical extravaganza that marks the Last Night of the Proms for the BBC, Proms in the Park, I look a few hundred yards north to Tyburn Hill.

And rainy holidays, and 'dying' on stage, don't seem so bad.

9 June 2013

MIGHT IS RIGHT?

Once more, 'research' stretches the fragile boundaries of our credibility with the information that strong men are likely to be right-wing, while the 10-stone weakling who used to get sand kicked in his face in those 'Charles Atlas' body-building ads of long ago is more likely to be a left-winger, peculiarly enough, on the redistribution of wealth. Although, I'd expect the weakling to be more interested in the redistribution of biceps and pecs, as he was in the old ads.

To the relief of all, these demented researchers found no link between upper-body strength and redistribution-of-wealth opinion among women. But after relentless dissection of bicep size and socio-economic status, the conclusion was drawn that men with higher upper-body strength were less likely to support left-wing policies. This inevitably leaves weightlifters, shot-putters, Schwarzenegger, Stallone, James Bond and the British and Irish Lions front row as right-wingers, even allowing for the fact that rugby props rarely break into more than a canter and will never be seen tearing down the left or, if it comes to that, right wing.

It looks as if Nigel Farage is missing a trick in not storming the gyms of Britain for more supporters of Ukip. Politically, these findings are dynamite: Ed Miliband, although only a chosen few will have seen him stripped and buffed, seems to fit the bill physically for the left-winger, and Ken Livingstone might have modelled for the role; but where does this research leave the burly Ed Balls? Again, we're not privy to the state of Nick Clegg's musculature, but fully clothed he looks suitably in the middle. However, even on the basis of a passing glance, some doubt must be cast on Vince Cable's credentials.

With continuing doubt and division reigning within the Conservatives, the physical condition of their party members might well prove the acid test of their true political leanings. Wet, dry or oiled, Boris Johnson has plenty of body, but we have to question how much is flab and how much solid muscle? Research shows that bulk alone does not a true right-winger make, and so far, no one who has arm-wrestled David Cameron has come forward. And a stiff workout with the barbells might well repay George Osborne and quell those doubters to the Right.

As ever, the royal family shows us the way. Spare and slim, like their father, the Princes William and Harry may not be obviously muscular, but nobody is going to kick any sand in either of their faces. Like all the family, there's not a hint of physical or political bias. We need have no fear of violent swings to the Left or Right from Her Majesty's Palace. But if there's anything to this loony research, we need to keep a beady eye on the boyos at the other palace. Eternal vigilance, the price of freedom, dictates that we look closely at those in the House with jackets that are too loose, or too tight, across the shoulders. Don't be deceived by fine words; these are the giveaway signs.

16 June 2013

STILL SMALL VOICES

As the weeds grow ever more rampant on the verges, and the hedges proliferate, lessening the visibility on every turn of our little roads and lanes – they themselves in turn more dangerous every day with a thousand potholes, cracks, rifts and general disintegration through the same lack of care and maintenance that allows the hedgerows to take over the world like triffids – the lonely cry of the council tax payer echoes fruitlessly throughout the land. For he knows all too well that he might as well be whistling into the wind.

'No answer!' comes the stern reply to any complaint made to district or county councils. 'Cock a deaf 'un' is their age-old policy. 'Ignore 'em, they'll get fed up complaining. Just sit tight. What do you have to do to get another cup of tea around here?'

The loyal reader will know to their cost how the blood rushes to my head every year about this time, and I foam at the mouth and carry on like one possessed at the blinding stupidity of the lifting of a 30 mph speed restriction on my local lane, just where it becomes more dangerous. And now, with the unrestricted growth of verge and hedgerow, even more so.

As far as the apparatchiks of district and county council are concerned, I am but a voice crying in the wilderness. 'For heaven's sake! How are we expected to get any work done if we pay attention to every little complaint? This brochure, explaining all that we do for the council tax payer, doesn't write itself, you know.'

It seems a shame that the voice of legitimate protest is ignored, if it's not expressed in sufficient numbers and, for real effectiveness, riotously. The G8 protesters of the other week in London certainly made their voices heard, even if it was at the expense of ordinary people trying to go about their business. The protests of the people in Cairo and Istanbul have ended in flames, tear gas and repressive brutality, but they have rung around the world, and will inevitably bring change.

They say that peaceful protest worked for India and Gandhi, but for years I have watched the Falun Gong sit in silent criticism of the Chinese government, on the pavement opposite the Chinese embassy in London, without ever even a responsive twitch of an embassy curtain. In my experience our county and district councils have nothing to learn from the Chinese about impassivity, so there's not much point my pitching my yurt on the pavement opposite the council offices, with my protests crudely painted on cardboard. Members of the public are slow to react, and are more likely to cross the road to avoid me rather than join in a concerted movement to storm the building, even in the inflammatory cause of overgrown hedgerows and broken roads.

So, who is there to hear the small voice of individual complaint?

Please don't mention the ballot box – democracy only works if you've got a big enough crowd behind you. Prayer is the only answer. My granny always lit a candle to St Jude. He's the patron saint of hopeless cases. Worth a try.

23 June 2013

. . . AND FAREWELL

And so, the wheat having been separated from the chaff, ten years of 'Wogan's World' have been harvested . . . But don't think that you're getting off that lightly. It's only the end of the beginning, not the other way around. As a Rothschild once said to me, 'It's hard to stamp out a weed.'

There's plenty more where that came from.

Throw another log on the fire . . .